P9-CKA-935

An UNSEEN ANGEL

An UNSEEN ANGEL

A Mother's Story of Faith, Hope, and Healing after SANDY HOOK

ALISSA PARKER

ENSIGN
PEAK

For Emilie
You helped me see the beautiful connections
that bind us together forever.

And for Madeline and Samantha
This book is my gift to you. I hope you always
remember the love you shared with your sister.

Photo on page 35 courtesy AP Photo/Julio Cortez.
Photo on page 38 courtesy AP Photo/Jessica Hill.
All other photographs courtesy of the author.

© 2017 Alissa Parker

All rights reserved. No part of this book may be reproduced in any form or by any means without permission in writing from the publisher, Ensign Peak®, at permissions@shadowmountain.com. The views expressed herein are the responsibility of the author and do not necessarily represent the position of Ensign Peak.

Visit us at shadowmountain.com

Library of Congress Cataloging-in-Publication Data
(CIP on file)
ISBN 978-1-62972-279-5

Printed in the United States of America
Edwards Brothers Malloy, Ann Arbor, MI

10 9 8 7 6 5 4 3 2 1

CONTENTS

~~~~~~

PROLOGUE

March 23, 2013
Newtown, Connecticut

I looked out the bay window of my living room and my heart started pounding. A grey Connecticut State Police SUV had just eased to a stop in the driveway. My husband, Robbie, put his arm around my shoulder, as if to say, *It's going to be all right.* But I wasn't all right—I was anxious, queasy, and frightened. It had been three months since twenty first-grade children and six adults had been killed by a lone gunman at Sandy Hook Elementary School. My daughter Emilie was one of those victims. Their investigations now complete, the police were here to return the clothes she had been wearing at the time of the shooting.

One of the officers, a woman I knew well by now, started down our stone walkway. Shortly after the shooting I had talked to her on the telephone about what Emilie had worn that day—a dark pink shirt, a pink pleated skirt with ruffles, pink leggings, and black and pink snow boots. Emilie loved pink, I told her. Many times since then she had respectfully walked me through the grim details of the police investigation, one of the hardest ordeals of my life. When the investigation concluded, I requested Emilie's personal items, and she promised to hand-deliver them to our home.

Robbie opened the front door and said hello. I expected the officer to hand me a sealed bag with the word EVIDENCE on it. Instead she was holding a child-sized trunk. It was white with pink polka dots, and it had a rounded lid fastened with a metal latch. She carried it by the pink rope handles on the sides. A note the size of a business card was tied to a pink bow on top.

She handed the trunk to Robbie, who removed the note, and we read:

> *How lucky I am to have something*
> *that makes saying good-bye so hard.*
> *—A.A. Milne*

Our eyes welled up. By the time we looked up to thank the officer, she was gone. We watched her drive off, then sat on our living-room sofa, the trunk resting on our laps. With sunlight streaming through the window, we looked at each other and, without saying a word, we each knew what the other was feeling—apprehension. *Are we really ready to see how our daughter was murdered?*

Robbie slowly opened the lid of the little trunk, and the fresh scent of laundry detergent emerged. Emilie's clothes were neatly folded. It was almost as if someone had tried to wash away all traces of that awful day. My eyes were immediately drawn to the item on top—a purple fleece scarf that my mother had made for Emilie just one week before the shooting. I had forgotten about it until I saw it in the trunk. My mind went back to that morning in December when I had stood in the living room with Emilie, wrapping the scarf around her neck and tying it in a knot before she headed for the bus stop. She had worn that scarf all week long. It was her way of adding a fashionable accent to her outfits.

Robbie removed it from the trunk and unfolded it, and instantly I convulsed. The scarf had six bullet holes. Nauseous, I took the scarf from Robbie and ran my index finger over the holes. Then I arranged it just as I had done that morning for Emilie. When I bunched up the fabric I realized that the six holes represented the trajectory of a single bullet passing through the folds of fleece wrapped around her neck. I realized that it was probably the shot that killed my child. I looked at Robbie and we cried.

In the aftermath of the shooting I was desperate to know the details of what had happened to Emilie. Facts, I desperately hoped, would lead to understanding, to the bleak necessity of closure. Still, I kept these facts at an emotional arm's length. For instance, I had chosen not to look at Emilie's body at the funeral home before the mortician dressed her for the closed-casket memorial service. My last memory of Emilie was a happy one of her innocently running for the school bus, and I refused to replace that sunny image of her with anything more disturbing. I got through each day by considering the violence in her classroom as something abstract. That was my coping mechanism. I didn't want to think too deeply about what happens when a semiautomatic rifle is used to fire round after round of ammunition into a classroom of first graders, so I blocked those images from my mind.

Going through Emilie's clothes in the chest presented me with the undeniable, concrete reality of what had happened to our daughter. There was nothing abstract about the frayed strands of fabric around the holes. No amount of laundry detergent could expunge the proof of violence. The other items in the trunk—especially her shirt, which was sprayed with holes—confirmed the unthinkable. One moment I was putting my little girl on the school bus at the end of our road. An hour later, a man that my daughter had never met—twenty-year-old Adam Lanza—entered her classroom, pointed a gun at her, and pulled the trigger. Again. And again. And again. There was no getting around that fact. My six-year-old daughter didn't simply pass away on December 14, 2012. She was brutally murdered in the second deadliest school shooting by a lone individual in American history.

※

Writing a book about losing Emilie wasn't something I had planned to do. To begin with, I'm very private and reserved. Also, after Emilie died I couldn't bear to think about what had happened to her, much less write about it. Nor, I believe, do most people want to read about something so sad. But violence, grief, and loss are not what this book is primarily about; at least, I prefer not to look at it that way. Although it contains tragedy, my story is ultimately not tragic. The story I feel compelled to share is one of help and healing. It is a story of how God's love and protection surrounded me during my darkest hour.

I have always believed that family is eternal, that we are bound with our loved ones by a tie that outlasts disaster and death. But when Emilie died, my faith in this principle was put to the ultimate test. I asked God again and again to help me feel Emilie's presence, to confirm that she still was with me and that our family was and is forever connected. In His own time, He gave me this reassurance. I was granted very sacred personal experiences that allowed me to see and feel Emilie in the small and simple occurrences of daily life. I have no doubt whatsoever that Emilie lives, that she is still a part of my family, and that we will be reunited in God's time.

As I have pondered my experiences in writing this book, I have come to realize how truly blessed I have been. I can clearly see that God was indeed faithful to His promises to me the day Emilie died. His help has radically changed my life. I have finally come to the understanding that Emilie's story is one of joy.

Emilie, filled with joy

Emilie had six wonderful years on this earth. She made every day beautiful. She saw the world in color and spent every moment she could trying to capture that beauty in her artwork to share with others. Through all the pain, I have come to feel this truth with every fiber in me: Emilie's was a beautiful life. I feel honored to have been a part of it. God loves Emilie, and, even now, Emilie has a happy life, even if it didn't follow my plan for her "happy endings."

This is her story.

Book I

BEFORE

MY FOREVER FAMILY

~~~~~~~~~~

I'll never forget the day in late summer of 2011 when Robbie and I first drove into Newtown, Connecticut. Robbie had recently applied for a physician's assistant position at Danbury Hospital. At first I was apprehensive. I'd never been to New England. It seemed so far away; so different from the West, where we had both grown up and where we felt comfortable. But I accompanied Robbie when he flew out for his job interview. This would be an adventure, I thought.

As part of the recruiting process, the hospital arranged for us to spend a day with a realtor, who showed us a number of communities near Danbury. When she drove us down Main Street in Newtown, it was love at first sight. Everything was so green—lush lawns and leafy oaks and maples. There was an old-fashioned general store. Historic homes with colonial architecture proudly displayed American flags. There were brick sidewalks, charming shops, flower boxes teeming with purple and pink petunias, and white church steeples poking through the trees. Everything was so quaint and refined. It looked like something out of a storybook.

Then the realtor took us to Sandy Hook, a village on the edge of town. In Utah, our home state, there aren't villages within towns, so this was a new concept for us. We were charmed, especially when the realtor pulled up in front of Sandy Hook Elementary School. She told us it was one of the best schools in the area. Robbie said it looked just like the school he had attended as a boy.

At the end of a long day, I pulled out the map the realtor had given us and drew a big circle around Newtown. I told Robbie that was where I wanted to live. After many years of schooling, medical rotations, and starter jobs, this seemed to be the perfect place for our wandering family to put down roots and start our "happily ever after."

✿

I first met Robbie Parker in middle school in Ogden, Utah. Tall and skinny, with long, gangly arms, Robbie was a good student, but he had the reputation for being funny and a bit of a flirt. For years we were great friends, but near the end of high school, things between us changed. I felt drawn to him, and he seemed to go out of his way to see me. We saw the world in the same way. We enjoyed being together and confided in each other. By the time I graduated, we were spending almost every day together. When Robbie left to serve a two-year mission for our church, our relationship deepened even further. Although we were far apart physically, we wrote each other every week

Our forever family

for two years, sharing our feelings and thoughts, discovering that we were compatible on a deeply spiritual level. By the time he came home, it was clear to both of us that we were meant to be together. Three months later, we were married.

We faced several years of undergraduate poverty together, working odd jobs to make ends meet while we studied and prepared for our future. Both of us looked forward to the time we could start a family. I longed to be a mother, but found that it would not be as simple as we hoped. After we struggled for two years to conceive, my first pregnancy ended in a heartbreaking miscarriage. Thankfully, a few months later I became pregnant again, and everything went smoothly this time. Our excitement grew as we prepared for our new arrival—a baby girl. I was determined that her room would not be the stereotypical pink, so I carefully sewed a patchwork quilt of purple and yellow for her crib.

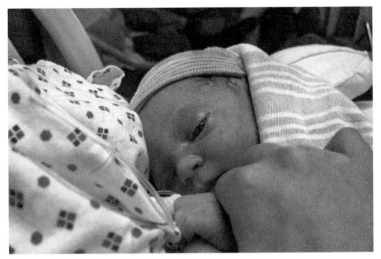

Baby Emilie

Our baby—Emilie—was born May 12, 2006. I brought her home from the hospital on Mother's Day. She was the perfect gift.

Emilie and I settled into a routine, getting to know each other as mother and daughter. With me, Robbie, and now Emilie, our little family felt like a precious, complete unit, surrounded and supported by the love and care of our friends and family. When Emilie was only a few months old, I had an experience that convinced me that the loving care of my family extended even beyond the bounds of this life and time.

My dad's father, my Grandpa Cottle, had always been one of my favorite people. He was funny, strong, and tenderhearted. My grandma had passed away a few years earlier, and my grandpa often joked about being ready to die so he could see her again. When I found out I was pregnant with Emilie, I teased him, "Now you'll have to stick around long enough to meet her!" He looked at me with a smirk and said, "Well, tell her to hurry up!" My grandpa passed away a month later, without having the chance to see Emilie.

One afternoon I sat on my couch with Emilie on my lap. She had just started smiling, and I couldn't get enough of her sweet little grin. I held her to my face while she touched my lips and we smiled at each other attentively. Suddenly Emilie's face turned to the side and her eyes focused intently on something next to me. I turned and tried to see what she was looking at. I saw nothing, but I watched her as she stared and began to grin and laugh. My heart pounded, and a swelling feeling filled my chest. There in that moment, I felt—*I knew*—that Grandpa was there with me, meeting my Emilie, just as we had joked about months earlier. Tears filled my eyes as I watched her continue to smile.

My experience with my grandpa convinced me that our loved ones who have passed on remain with us in spirit. It was intense and powerful, and yet at the same time it was incredibly private. Whenever I tried to explain the significance of the experience to someone else, my words could not re-create it. It was special because of the way I felt in my heart. That feeling, and the sacred emotion it left in my heart and memory, was special only to me. I knew in my bones that heaven was closer than I had ever imagined, and so were those loved ones who were gone.

As Emilie grew, she was a joy. The first word she spoke was *happy.* I entered her bedroom one morning and found her standing in her crib, pointing at her favorite toy—a stuffed mouse. The word *happy* came out of her mouth. She was only five months old. I couldn't think of a more appropriate word for her to say. I handed her the mouse, and she repeated the word again. From then on the mouse's name was Happy.

By the time Emilie was nine months old, she was speaking in short sentences. She was very verbal, very early. She was also unusually obedient. When she outgrew her crib and transitioned to a toddler bed, I was a little worried. She had been such a great sleeper, and I wondered if having the freedom to get in and out of bed would make bedtime a disaster. The first night she slept in her "big girl bed," I explained to her that she had to stay in her bed, and when she woke up in the morning she should call me. I would come into her room and get her, just as I always did. I kissed her and gave her a hug and hoped this wasn't the beginning of a long, sleepless night.

The next morning I opened Emilie's door and found her sitting on her bed, waiting for me as always. She jumped up and ran to me, excited that she was now officially a big girl!

Robbie was accepted into a graduate physician assistants' program in Oregon, and shortly afterwards, we gave birth to our second daughter, Madeline. We packed up our belongings and set out for an adventure in the Pacific Northwest. It was beautiful, with lush trees, amazing hiking, ocean beaches, and many free family activities. Since Robbie was consumed with his schooling, I spent a lot of time exploring with the girls. We fell in love with Oregon immediately.

Emilie loved books, and we spent hours reading together. She quickly picked up on things, so I began doing preschool at home with her every day. She had an excitement for learning and loved to ask questions. One morning shortly after we had begun our preschool, Emilie looked up at me and asked, "Mom, are you sick?" I had been feeling sick for a few days without getting any better. I wondered . . . could I be pregnant again? It seemed impossible, since Madeline was only six months old! I wasn't ready for another baby! But the positive reading on the pregnancy test proved to me that it was indeed possible. I did the math and realized I would be having three babies in less than three years.

The thought of this overwhelmed me. I wanted to be happy, but I was terrified. Robbie had similar concerns, but he told me he had a strong feeling this was what God wanted. He later explained that as he stood there looking at me with the positive pregnancy test in my hand, before he could react or even develop a thought on his own, he had an impression telling him, "It doesn't matter what you think, this is right. This is how it is supposed to happen." He said that although logically he knew this was crazy, he felt at peace because there were bigger plans at play than our own. His confidence helped calm my anxiety, but it didn't necessarily make things easier as I went through another pregnancy—this time with a two-year-old, a baby just learning to walk, and a husband who was busy studying. It was crazy and chaotic. At times I still had doubts. That was, up until the moment I saw our sweet baby Samantha for the first time. Immediately, she was the perfect fit. We used to joke she was the eye of the storm in our home. Everything around her was loud and crazy, and she just watched contentedly.

Two weeks after she was born, we packed up again and began the next stretch of our family's adventure—rotations! For the second year of PA school, Robbie had to do ten different medical rotations, each lasting six weeks, at ten different practices, which could be anywhere in the United States. Together, we hit the road again.

Moving around so often bonded our family. We were usually not in any one place long enough to make friends, so we filled that void with each other. While Robbie worked long hours, Emilie was often the only person I had to talk to for days at a time. We made the best of it by spending most of our time working creatively on art projects together. Coloring, painting, photography, sewing, and drawing were things we loved to do together. Emilie was a gifted artist. She loved to pour her ideas and thoughts out on paper. It helped me see the world through her eyes.

One of Robbie's last rotations took us to the Oregon coast, where we lived in a little rental house right next to the ocean. Every morning I would pack Samantha in a backpack carrier, take Madeline and Emilie by the hand, and walk to the beach. Madeline would plop on the sand and dig holes, and Emilie and I would sneak up on seagulls and scare them into flight.

It was often a challenge raising three little girls so close in age. Their demands on my attention were great. Emilie was an amazing helper, eager to assist me in any way possible. If Samantha needed a new diaper, she would get one for me. If Madeline needed help getting a toy, Emilie was there to reach it for her. Her younger sisters looked up to Emilie; she was the one with the big ideas and the most creative projects. Madeline and Samantha would often fight for her attention. If one of her sisters was upset, Emilie would take her in her arms and whisper, "It's okay. It's okay."

Emilie had grown to be a happy little girl with bright blue

Madeline, Emilie, and Samantha

eyes, set wide apart, and a crown of light blonde hair that she liked to wear long, almost to her waist. By the end of the day, her hair was always wild and tangled, a nightmare to brush. She had a distinct "Parker nose," which was wider than mine and sprinkled with light freckles for which we made up silly names. She named them after princesses; her favorite freckle was called Rose. She spoke with a cute little lisp, which I secretly hoped she wouldn't outgrow, at least for a while.

Emilie was a confident girl. She was three when she declared she would no longer wear anything but dresses. No pants, no skirts—only dresses. This phase lasted until she was four and a half. During that time she also insisted on wearing a crown and telling everyone she met that her name was Sleeping Beauty. Adults would laugh the way they do when kids say something cute. Then they'd say: "What's your real name?"

She would respond sternly, "Sleeping Beauty!"

Once, when we attended church for the first time in a new town, the leader of our new congregation introduced our family by reading our names over the pulpit. After saying Emilie's name, he added: "But she told me to call her Sleeping Beauty." The congregation chuckled. Emilie just beamed.

By the time Robbie finished school with a degree in Physician Assistant Studies, we had lived in several places in Oregon, Washington, and Montana. Then he took his first job in New Mexico.

Emilie's school in New Mexico was about a half mile away from our home. Every day I would load Madeline and Samantha into our double stroller and walk Emilie to and from school. I loved this time with Emilie because it was her time to tell me all about her day without any interruptions. Pushing the large stroller around prevented me from holding Emilie's hand, which was one of my favorite things to do with my girls. I would often tell Emilie how much I missed holding her hand as we walked. One day, while we were waiting at a red light, Emilie reached over and grabbed my hand and said, "I was thinking we could hold hands when we have to stop at the light. That way you could take a turn holding my hand! Then you don't have to miss it so much." I laughed and told her what a good idea that was. Holding hands at the red light became part of our routine.

On Emilie's first day of kindergarten in New Mexico, she discovered that her name had a somewhat unusual spelling. She came home from school and reported that there was another girl with the same name, but hers was spelled *Emily.* "Why is mine spelled E-M-I-L-I-E?"

Robbie explained that his name also ended in *I-E,* instead of the more traditional spelling of *Robby.* "We spelled your name with an *I-E* so you and I could be special together," he told her.

At that moment she decided she liked being different. From then on she made a point of telling people how to spell her name, with an *I-E* like her dad's name.

One of Emilie's best friends at school was Arianna, a little girl so shy she rarely spoke and had never had a play date. Emilie didn't mind her shyness. We used to joke that Emilie sought out shy friends because it gave her more scope to do all the talking.

It was around this time that I noticed a real difference in Emilie's hands. Instead of the soft, smooth hand I was used to, her hands were beginning to feel hard and coarse, much rougher than the hands of other kids her age. As I examined them more carefully, I noticed that she was developing calluses, especially on her right hand. I thought about all the hours each day she spent creating artwork. Her bag of markers, crayons, and oil pastels would go with her everywhere. In the back of our minivan she kept a large tray that had pockets for her art supplies. We made it a habit to provide a large supply of paper for her. It wasn't uncommon for her to go through a notebook a day.

She did a lot of artwork at night, too. In addition to being an early riser, Emilie tended to stay up late. It was as if her internal clock was just different. In order to instill good habits, I would insist that she go to bed at bedtime, but I allowed her to sit up and color or draw until she got sleepy. She would literally spend two to three hours each night doing artwork in bed. Most nights her light would still be on when I went to bed.

Many mornings I would wake up and find a colored picture outside my bedroom door with the words *To Mom* written on it. There would also be colored pictures that said *To Dad*,

To Samantha, and *To Madeline.* And whenever she thought she had done something wrong, she would color a picture and write the words *I'm sorry* on it. It was her way of apologizing.

I planned for our first Christmas in New Mexico to be really special. Christmas was always a big deal in our home, and I often made many of our kids' gifts for them. Living a student lifestyle for so many years had taught me to be thrifty. Now that Robbie had a job, I decided I was going to splurge a little and buy Emilie an American Girl doll for Christmas. It arrived with blue eyes and long blonde hair, just like Emilie's. Excitedly, I hid it in our closet, and I secretly sewed clothes and accessories for the doll after the girls were in bed at night. On Christmas morning, I was not disappointed when Emilie opened up her doll. She screamed and hugged the box over and over. She named the doll *Emily,* with a "y."

For all our good times in New Mexico, we knew that we would not be there for long. Soon, plans were in motion for us to make the move to Connecticut.

Robbie had accepted an offer to work at Danbury Hospital in the neonatal intensive care unit. The job seemed ideal, the answer to our prayers. After years of working long hours and late nights, Robbie was offered a schedule that would allow him to spend much more time with the girls and me. He had waded through state licensing requirements and background checks for months, but now we had to move quickly. The girls went to Utah with my mom while Robbie and I drove a moving truck from New Mexico to Connecticut. We unloaded most of our stuff into a storage unit there. We took the bare minimum—clothes and personal items—to a temporary rental in New Fairfield, where we planned to live just until we found a place in Newtown.

While Robbie started working, I flew back to Utah to retrieve the girls. On January 9, 2012, I boarded a flight with them in Salt Lake City. It was my first time flying alone with all three girls. I was a little overwhelmed, especially when we changed planes in Denver. The second leg of the flight was crowded, and I couldn't find four seats together. A woman saw my distress and began asking people to change seats in order to open space for us. I settled into a middle seat between Samantha and Madeline. That left Emilie to sit across the aisle next to the woman who had helped us. She was traveling with her fiancé. I was afraid Emilie would talk their ears off and annoy them.

The flight was four hours long, and Emilie chattered the entire time, but the couple never complained. In particular, the woman took a personal interest in Emilie. Emilie was animated as always, but so was her seatmate and new friend. They both chatted off and on the entire flight as Emilie colored lots of pictures for her.

I felt disappointed that I never got the woman's name. She and her fiancé were lifesavers. When I spotted them in the baggage claim area, I introduced them to Robbie as the couple who had helped me on the flight. They shook Robbie's hand. Then the woman referred to Emilie as "my girl." As we said good-bye, Emilie waved. I figured I would never see that woman again.

❧

I enrolled Emilie in kindergarten at Consolidated School in New Fairfield. I worried about her joining a new class in the middle of a school year, but she instantly fit in. Making friends came easily to Emilie. Within the first week she came home from school excited and talking fast.

"Mom, there's this boy at school and his first name is Parker. And he's new too. We decided to get married. And he's going to have the same last name as me. He's going to be called Parker Parker. Isn't that funny?"

I laughed as I tried to explain that the boy's last name usually doesn't change when he gets married. Undeterred, she assured me that his would.

Parker's family had moved to New Fairfield around the same time as we had. Unlike Emilie, Parker was quiet and shy. The two of them bonded quickly. She even made him a necklace out of colored beads that he wore to school.

A couple weeks after telling me that she and Parker were going to marry, Emilie came home from school with a drawing of a house. It was pink and blue. Her favorite color was pink; his was blue. They had colored it together. "This is the house we're going to build after we get married," she told me. Not long after that, they started referring to each other as "my love."

I don't remember referring to any boy as *my love* when I was in kindergarten, but Emilie was very expressive. Her kindergarten teacher, Mrs. Brown, picked up on that right away and essentially took Emilie under her wing. Mrs. Brown had flowing dark hair and a pretty smile. She dressed stylishly and often wore a scarf in class. Emilie had been designing dresses for her American Girl doll, and Mrs. Brown became a bit of a role model for her. She often told me that Mrs. Brown was a "fancy" dresser and she wanted to dress like her.

We were in New Fairfield for only three months before finding a house in Newtown. Unfortunately, Emilie had to

Emilie and Mrs. Brown

change schools again. She wasn't very excited about that. She especially didn't want to say good-bye to Parker and Mrs. Brown. On her last day at Consolidated School, I showed up near the end of the school day and spent some time in her classroom. She was wearing a paper crown that said "Super Kid." Basically, Mrs. Brown had designated the day in honor of Emilie. She even presented Emilie with a handmade book called *Emilie's Consolidated School Family.* Each pink-construction-paper page contained laminated pictures of Emilie and her classmates, including one of Emilie and Parker that had been taken on Parker's birthday. The last page contained a picture of Emilie sitting on Mrs. Brown's lap, Emilie wearing a princess crown, Mrs. Brown beaming. She had written a note:

My Sweet Emilie—
   You will shine at your new school! We all love you and will miss you.

                Mrs. Brown

Before we left that day, Mrs. Brown pulled me aside. "Emilie is gifted," she whispered. "Whatever she wants to do in life, she'll do. If she wants to be a doctor, she'll be a doctor. She's going places."

I didn't know what to say.

She made me promise to stay in touch. "I want to know what happens to this little girl," she said.

As we drove Emilie home from Consolidated School for the last time, she said: "I still want to marry Parker."

✤

It was April, and that weekend we moved into a small house on Country Squire Lane in Newtown. It needed a lot of work on the inside, but it was what we could afford. I promised Emilie that we would construct an arts and crafts room just for her in the basement. That gave her something to look forward to.

Emilie was both nervous and excited the first time we entered the doors at Sandy Hook Elementary. After taking a walking tour of the school and meeting some kids in her class, she was eager to make new friends. She quickly adjusted to her new school while we fixed up our house.

My parents flew out to help us with a few projects on the house. The timing worked out perfectly, since my dad was coming out to run in the Boston Marathon. My dad quickly assessed our house, grabbed a hammer, and set to work. I had a long to-do list, and he was never one to be idle. Robbie picked up a lot of extra shifts at the hospital to help fund our renovations, and that left me to be my dad's assistant. I loved it. We worked side by side tearing down walls, building closets, and rewiring electrical circuits. We didn't talk much as we worked, but I felt close to him as we got lost in what we were doing. After a week of renovating, the whole family drove up to Boston and cheered my dad's marathon run with homemade signs (Emilie's idea).

After my dad's visit, we finished the rest of the renovations ourselves. When the time came to decorate Emilie's room, all she wanted was her favorite color, pink—pink walls, pink curtains, pink bedding, pink, pink, pink. After lots of negotiations, we decided to do grey walls with pops of pink in the bedding, curtains, and furniture. Finally, we accented the grey walls with a group of stenciled flowers in pink, black, and blue. Emilie loved her new room.

By the end of summer 2012, we were finally done. We felt so blessed to have our first real home, a great job opportunity for Robbie, and a wonderful new community for the girls to grow up in. After all our work and wandering, we felt we had earned our little piece of "happily ever after."

2

GOING ON AHEAD

~~~~~~

We were just settling into our new home when Emilie entered the first grade at Sandy Hook. Peace, contentment, and optimism seemed to be all around. But that peace was shattered by a phone call just a few days after school started. When I picked up the phone, I heard my mother crying on the other end of the line.

"What's going on?" I asked.

"There has been an accident. All I know is that your dad fell off his bike and is now being airlifted to a nearby hospital. I don't know how bad it is yet. I don't know anything! I will call you as soon as I get to the hospital and find out what is going on."

My father was an avid cyclist. On that morning he had joined in the LOTOJA Classic, the longest single-day USA

My dad on his bicycle

Cycling–sanctioned race in the country. At 6:00 a.m. he was among 1,500 cyclists who pedaled out of Logan, Utah, heading for the finish line 206 miles away in Jackson Hole, Wyoming. This was one of my dad's favorite races. It was extremely difficult, but that was exactly why he couldn't resist. Every year he said it was going to be his last race, but without fail he would sign up the following year. I spoke with him on the phone the night before the race, and he told me that he hadn't been feeling good about racing this year. I told him maybe he should back out, and he shrugged it off, saying he could never do that.

I later found out that after crossing into Idaho, my dad was going about forty-five miles per hour down the mountain when another cyclist passed him and accidentally clipped his wheel, sending him crashing headfirst to the ground. He sustained multiple fractures to his facial bones and a traumatic brain injury.

I flew to Utah the next morning to be with my family. After arriving at the hospital, I learned that my dad's brain was swollen and he was confined to an intensive care unit. His eyes were swollen shut and his entire body was covered in cuts and deep bruises. I hardly recognized him. Shocked by his condition, I leaned in close so that he could get a good look at my face and asked, "Dad, do you know my name?" He opened his one eye and simply replied, "Yes."

I prayed that he would live. All of us did. Day after day we sat in his room quietly waiting. He had been so fit and strong before the accident. Surely, I kept telling myself, he would pull through. Other than his daily therapies, he slept most of the day. There were many times I found myself just staring at him and having the distinct feeling he wasn't there. It was as if his body lay healing and his soul went off somewhere else. I asked my mom if she ever had the same feeling and she responded, "Many times."

Luckily, his progress was fast, and we started to see glimpses of his personality returning, which gave us hope that he would recover well. After two weeks of hospitalization, he was well enough to transfer to a rehabilitation center. I flew home, confident that my dad would make an amazing recovery. He was a fighter. But as soon as I got home, I received the bad news that, due to the lack of space at an appropriate rehab facility, he had been sent to an assisted living center. It was essentially a nursing home that wasn't equipped to provide the around-the-clock care he needed. My mom spent all her nights trying to sleep in a recliner next to his bed. To help her, Robbie flew to Utah and spent his nights with my dad. Late one night, my dad tried to stand up from his bed, and his leg gave out. Robbie lunged, but not in time. My dad hit his head on the floor. His brain started bleeding, and he slipped into a coma.

I flew to Utah again and was there with my whole family on September 29 when my dad took his last breath. My mother had made the excruciating decision not to artificially prolong his life. We tearfully watched as the life-support machines were turned off, and we silently waited and listened to the heart monitor chirping. Gradually, the beats became further and further apart. I held on to his hand tighter. And after only fifteen short minutes, his heart stopped and he left this world. He was only sixty-two.

The sudden absence of my dad plunged me into shock. Life without him seemed inconceivable. He had always been my rock, the one I went to in times of trouble. He had taught me so much about life and about unconditional love. Our relationship served as the foundation for my relationship with God. Despite the mistakes I made or the problems I had, my dad was there to support me. I always felt comfortable going to him with my doubts and struggles in life. At those times when I didn't live up to my own expectations, he was always there to pick me up. He had taught me to have that same trusting relationship with God, to depend on Him in my times of need. I had a hopeful faith that God would be there to support me, but with the pain I was feeling, I wondered if that kind of help existed. And, if it really did, how could I access it?

I thought back to the influence my parents had had throughout my life. My parents were practicing Mormons, like

With my dad at the Boston Marathon

most of the people in our community. The Church of Jesus Christ of Latter-day Saints was a big part of my upbringing. Many of my closest friends at school attended my congregation. But my two best friends growing up were my mom and dad.

My father was a charismatic man who was often the center of attention, a gifted storyteller and a natural leader. He was often asked to speak at funerals. I remember listening to him speak about his own firm belief in a glorious afterlife, and as a child I accepted every word without question.

I clearly recollect one funeral at which my dad spoke when I was only seven or eight years old. The young son of close family friends had died suddenly and unexpectedly. In his remarks, my dad testified confidently to the heartbroken family about heaven and the opportunities their son would still have to grow to his full potential on the other side. I tried to envision what that heaven might be like and if it were true that there would be a chance for that child to experience the things he missed in this life. My dad's faith in such matters was strong.

My mom had a different personality—reserved, thoughtful, and very patient. She generally didn't offer advice until it was asked of her, but when she did speak, she was very intelligent and always had an insightful response that went right to the heart of any important matter. She led by her quiet, steady example.

Because of my parents' examples, I always had a close connection, even from an early age, with God. I knew He heard my prayers. I knew He loved me. I often had questions about spiritual things, and when I did, I turned to my parents for help. Their belief in God was unwavering, and they understood me even when I didn't understand myself. They taught me some lessons that enabled me to get through tough times.

When I was eleven, I felt depressed for the first time. I had always been a sensitive child, and the many bad things I was hearing in the news—war, rape, murder, and suffering—began to accumulate in my mind and weigh heavily on me. How, I wondered, could goodness win out when there was so much evil in the world? I felt a sense of hopelessness and sadness that affected my behavior and would not go away.

My parents noticed, but they didn't say anything about it until after my cousin Lora came over to spend the night one weekend. During our sleepovers, we usually stayed up late watching movies, giggling, and talking well past midnight.

On this particular occasion, however, I didn't feel like talking. Instead, I rebuffed my cousin, ignoring her completely. I didn't mean to. I just didn't feel good about myself.

The next day my father sat me down and asked what was bothering me. I told him I didn't really know. I was just sad. He pulled out the Bible and read 1 Corinthians 10:13: "There hath no temptation taken you but such as is common to man: but God is faithful, who will not suffer you to be tempted above that ye are able; but will with the temptation also make a way to escape, that ye may be able to bear it."

He asked me if I knew what that verse meant. I didn't. So he explained it by repeating the part about God not allowing individuals to be tempted beyond their ability to withstand. Then he applied that principle to me.

"Heavenly Father will never give you something you can't handle," he told me. "And when trouble comes, He will give you everything you need to overcome any challenge. He will never abandon you."

I didn't realize it at the time, but my dad was teaching me an important principle that would help me with challenges I would encounter throughout my life. I never forgot his words.

My mom also did something to help me. A few days after the sleepover, she came to my bedroom with a present. It was a framed picture that she had drawn of three balloons floating together in the sky. Beneath the balloons she had written in calligraphy: *RISE ABOVE IT.* She told me that those three words always helped her whenever she felt depressed. Up to that point, I had never known that my mother had moments of sadness. It helped me to know I wasn't alone. The picture gave me the reassurance that I could get through sadness because my mother got through it, and that it was my choice to let go of darkness and reach for light in my life.

I needed those two messages—*God doesn't give us more than we can handle* and *Rise above it*—more at the time of my father's death than I ever had before. This kind of misery and sadness was new to me. To distract myself from the pain, I worked tirelessly with my siblings on the funeral arrangements. I told myself I had to be strong for my mother. After leaving the funeral home at the end of a long day of making difficult decisions, my mom and I sat in the car parking lot exhausted. There were so many emotions running through my head, but the one I was feeling the most was anger. I was angry at the biker who had collided with my dad, angry at the VA rehab that didn't have room, and angry that I no longer could be with him. As I looked over at my mom, I realized I needed help dealing with these strong emotions.

"Mom," I finally asked, "how are you feeling about all this? Are you feeling angry at all?"

"A little," she sighed. "But I keep going back to the day he died. I had gone into his room alone and asked him if I was supposed to let go, telling him I was having a hard time with the decision. I had a strong feeling of peace come over me—the first time since his accident that I had felt peace. I knew it was the right thing to do."

She paused for a minute, trying to push back the tears. "I remember when we lived in California and we would go on family bike rides together. Every time, your dad would take off in the lead and all you kids would follow. I would stay in the back so that I could see everyone and make sure you were all safe and yell out if you were going the wrong way. In many ways, that was how we raised you. Now Dad has gone on ahead to heaven, and we are all following. And it is my role to make sure you all make it back safely. It's my job to yell out if you need a course correction. But we are all trying to make it back to be with him again."

❦

The funeral was difficult. A family friend sang my father's favorite song, "Bring Him Home" from *Les Misérables.* My dad had indeed gone home, leaving me bereft of the constant strength I had relied on for so many years. Would I be able to rise above the sadness?

It wasn't until after the funeral, when I returned to Connecticut, that I really had a chance to catch my breath. I thought deeply about what my mother had said to me. As I processed the emotions I was feeling about the senselessness of my father's death, I kept thinking about a conversation I had had with him many years earlier. He had just learned that one of his closest friends had stomach cancer and that his chances for survival were slim. My dad was angry at the injustice of the situation. His friend, through no fault of his own, was now fighting for his life. My dad wondered, *How could God let this happen? How could it be just?*

"But," he told me, "I finally realized that God wouldn't be God if he took my friend's burden away. By being here on this earth, we are exposed to many difficulties not caused by anything we have done. To take away hardships, or to limit one's agency to make disastrous choices, is against God's way. What God *can* do is support us and help us grow stronger so we can carry those burdens. He isn't to blame. He is our hope."

I wondered whether I could forgive those people I blamed

for my dad's death. There were a lot of prayers for peace and a lot of tears—not just from me, but from my whole family. Robbie was filled with guilt. My dad had been like a second father to him. Emilie struggled with my dad's death as well; she'd had a close relationship with her grandfather. We lived far away, but whenever we visited, he would spend a lot of one-on-one time with her. He would play games with her, take her to the park, and at bedtime read story after story to her. I remember once walking in on their bedtime reading only to find my dad with a crown on his head doing his best impersonation of a princess voice.

One morning Emilie and I were alone at the kitchen table sipping hot chocolate. She started crying and said, "I miss Grandpa! I miss him so much."

"I miss him too," I told her.

"What if something bad happened to me, and I died too?"

"Oh, Em, that would kill me," I said. "I would never let that happen. Ever. I promise."

The only thing that helped me forget the sadness of losing my dad was spending time with my girls. I especially loved our Friday movie nights, when Robbie worked late and I cuddled up with the girls to watch a video. This often led to a fight between Madeline and Samantha over who got to lie next to me on the couch, so I would lie on my side and one of them would lie in front of me while the other lay on top of me. Emilie also loved to snuggle with me, but she was content to sit quietly behind my legs, wrapping them around herself like a nest. Deep down, I knew we would get through our sadness the same way we managed everything—tightly knit together.

3

THE UNTHINKABLE

~~~~~~~~~~

While we were traveling back and forth to Utah because of my dad's accident, we had missed a lot of events with Emilie's new first-grade class. We missed back-to-school night, where we could meet her new teacher and the other parents and students in Emilie's class. Emilie missed her class picture, something that really bothered her when she got her copy of the picture to bring home. She told me how much she liked her class and followed me around the house as I cleaned, pointing to each child in the picture and telling me all about each one. I had been so consumed with my father's death that I hadn't been as involved as I would normally have been in Emilie's class.

One event that we were able to attend that fall was Emilie's parent-teacher conference. On that night, we had been pleased with Emilie's teacher and charmed with the school. It seemed so old-fashioned and quaint, reminding Robbie of his own elementary school. As we walked from the front door to Emilie's room, the third classroom from the entrance, I felt a tiny twinge of anxiety. *If anyone came into the school intent on harming someone, Emilie would be vulnerable,* I thought. But I quickly dismissed the feeling.

🦋

December 14, 2012. I was in bed, half asleep, when I felt Emilie crawling on top of me. It was just after seven, and Robbie had already left for work. I opened my eyes to see Emilie's face inches from mine. She was smiling, and the sunlight streaming through the window glowed around her golden blonde hair. "Hi, Mom!"

It was such a great way to wake up. "You are so beautiful," I told her.

She rolled off me, and we snuggled in the blankets. Lying there, I thought to myself: *I wish we could just stay here all day.* The moment was so perfect that I really didn't want it to end.

But after a few minutes, I led her to her room, and she tried on outfits while I sat on her bed. She finally settled on an all-pink outfit. Satisfied, she turned to me.

"Mom, I have something to show you."

I yawned. "What is it?"

She pointed to the flowers we had stenciled on the wall above her bed. "Do you see these two flowers, Mom? One is pink with a black center and the other is black with a pink center. Don't you see it, Mom? There's a connection! If you look around, you will see there are connections everywhere! Isn't it exciting? Everything is connected!"

Emilie was always so energetic in the morning, but I was

Emilie's room with the flowers on the wall

just the opposite. Staring at her wall, I sensed I wasn't fully grasping what she was trying to tell me, but I smiled and nodded my head. I turned my attention to the other girls. Before long we were off to the bus stop.

At the bus stop, we had a routine. Emilie would kiss me and say good-bye before boarding the bus; then she'd look back after climbing on board to wave good-bye. But on this particular morning the routine was interrupted. Madeline wandered off and got stuck on a hill by the roadside just as the bus was pulling up. I hugged Emilie, saying a quick "I love you," and then ran to help Madeline, trying to free her in time to catch Emilie's wave. When I turned around, Emilie was running toward the bus. Watching her run with her golden hair flying wildly behind her, I realized that I hadn't even brushed her hair that morning. For some reason, she didn't look up and wave to me when the bus drove off. It was the first time she had ever forgotten to wave.

Oh well, I told myself. *It's just this once.*

After dropping Madeline off at preschool, I went Christmas shopping with my three-year-old, Samantha. We ended up in Danbury at a secondhand store for kids called "Once Upon a Time." I picked up a bag of Legos for Emilie and had just tucked it under my arm when my cell phone rang. It was 9:45. An automated message indicated that there had been a shooting at a Newtown school. It was unclear which school was involved.

A sick feeling formed in my stomach and my hands started shaking. A shooting?

I told myself, *It's okay. I am sure she is fine. It most likely happened at the high school, or maybe the middle school. She has to be fine.*

I called Robbie at the hospital and learned that he had just received the same call from the school. He had run to his break room and turned on the news to see if he could find out anything. He told me the shooting was at Sandy Hook Elementary. I immediately thought of the location of Emilie's classroom. *She's in the front of the school! The doors don't lock! There is nothing to stop someone with a gun!*

I tried not to panic as I grabbed Samantha and headed for the car. I picked up Madeline from her preschool first and then headed for Sandy Hook. There was only one road leading to the school, and by this time it was choked with traffic. I called my mom and began to tell her about what had happened. "Her classroom is at the front of the school!" I cried. My mom told me that on the news they were reporting that a teacher had been shot in the foot and the shooter might have been her son. *A domestic problem. Okay, it was a domestic dispute that had nothing to do with the kids.* I imagined how scared Emilie must be. I felt the urge to comfort her immediately, but my car was barely moving. I could see ambulances rushing toward the school, and I wondered why so many were coming if only one person had been shot. *Were there more?* My heart beat faster as I considered the awful possibility that others might have been injured.

After minutes passed, I realized that no ambulances were leaving the school. I had so many questions and I felt frantic. *What is going on?* I finally reached the long driveway that led to the school parking lot, but it was blocked off by police officers. From the road I couldn't see the school, but what I did see was utter chaos. The road was jammed with cars, emergency vehicles, and people. I parked four blocks from the school and started running with my girls toward the flashing lights. There was a firehouse next to the school's driveway, and I could see people running in and out—parents, children, police officers, EMTs, teachers, firemen. The whole area was in complete disarray.

I ran into a teacher, who told me that the first graders had been the first students evacuated. I was sent to an empty room at the rear of the firehouse to wait for Emilie. Soon more parents arrived, then more. Before long the room was full of parents, all of us waiting for news about our missing children. I felt incredibly sick. I couldn't think of anything other than finding my daughter. Madeline and Samantha were next to me, struggling to sit still. My neighbor Stephanie, who also had a child at the school, called my cell phone and asked if Emilie was all right. I explained that she hadn't been accounted for and that I was waiting for her in the firehouse. Minutes later Stephanie showed up and asked if I would like her to take my girls home with her. I was filled with relief and gratitude for my sweet friend and told her how much I would appreciate that. As I watched her

Aerial photo of the Sandy Hook area after the shooting

take the hands of my two little blonde girls and lead them out the door, I couldn't help hoping that someone might be holding Emilie's hand right now and leading her back to me.

I felt so helpless and so alone. Robbie was stuck at the hospital, which had been put into lockdown as a result of the shooting. I looked around the room without recognizing a single face. I was a wreck. Then someone touched my shoulder, and I looked up to see Stephanie again. She explained that her husband had taken the girls so that she could come back and stay with me. I hugged her and thanked her again. She asked if there was anything she could do, and I immediately handed her my cell phone and asked her to help me reply to some texts. My hands were shaking so badly it had become impossible for me to use it. Stephanie ended up staying with us for hours that day, quietly lending her support.

Hours passed without an update. The room was filled with

frightened parents; it was difficult to look at them because the same emotions I was feeling were etched on their stricken faces. I hated that we were all trapped together in this cold, institutional room. For some reason, I kept obsessing about how I hadn't brushed Emilie's hair that morning. *If only I could brush her hair,* I told myself over and over.

Eventually, state troopers entered the room. One approached me and started asking questions about Emilie.

"Can you tell me what she was wearing?" he said.

I described her outfit: pink shirt, pink pleated skirt with ruffles, pink leggings, and pink and black snow boots.

"Do you have a picture of her?"

My hands were still shaking so badly I had trouble scrolling to an image of Emilie on my phone. The trooper looked at it. But he never looked at me. He never made eye contact. When he wasn't looking at his notepad, he stared past me. I feared the worst. Could she be dead? Was she gone? I tried to push those thoughts out of my mind.

Sometime in the early afternoon, an officer from the state police told us that twenty children were dead, but he didn't reveal any of their names. We were also led to believe that a handful of children were injured and had been taken to the hospital for treatment.

Robbie finally arrived moments after the latest update. As soon as I told him the news, I felt my chest constrict so tightly that I began to gasp for air. Robbie hugged me and tried to comfort me, but I fought for air more and more desperately. I heard Robbie say, "Alissa, you're having a panic attack! You need to breathe deeply!" My face went completely pale and an EMT came running over to me. "I can't feel my hands!" I blurted out between gasps for air. They took my coat off and laid me on the ground. All the bottled-up emotion I had been suppressing came flowing out of me, and I felt myself on the verge of hysteria. The EMT placed an oxygen mask on my face and began checking all my vitals. Robbie leaned over me, inches away from my face. "Alissa. I can't do this alone. They want to take you to the hospital, but I need you. I need you here with me. You need to calm down and breathe slowly." The thought of leaving without knowing what had happened to Emilie convinced me he was right. I tried to focus on my breathing—in and out, in and out. I needed to know if she could possibly still be alive. She might be one of the children who had been taken to the hospital. That was my only hope.

By 2:30 p.m. priests, nuns, and other clergy were on the scene, and I could hear many of them praying aloud over and over again. By this time, my own feelings had boiled to anger. I wanted information. I needed to know what had happened. Finally, around 3:30, Connecticut Governor Dan Malloy entered the room. I was physically exhausted and emotionally spent. The governor started talking as if none of our children had survived. I felt my anger growing as the governor spoke. I was fed up with the lack of information.

"What about the kids who went to the hospital?" I said. "What's their status?"

He then confirmed our worst fears, that all the children were dead. None of them had survived.

Everything around me began moving in slow motion. I was hot, and the room felt like it was shrinking. Again, I felt that I couldn't breathe.

"I have to get out of here," I told Robbie. "I need to leave now!"

I broke for the side door and pushed it open. Robbie followed. We ended up outside, behind the firehouse. Disoriented, we headed for the road in search of our car. We ran right into a pack of journalists and photographers who were set up in the firehouse parking lot. I'd had no idea the media were so close. Suddenly photographers were in our face, taking pictures. A fireman saw us being hounded and came to our rescue. "Hey!" he shouted at the press. "Back away! Back away!"

Confused, I shielded my eyes, and Robbie steadied me as we trudged toward our car. We got in, and I was panting and crying and trembling. "She's gone," I said.

It was the first time we had been alone all afternoon.

"What do we do now?" I said.

Leaving the firehouse with Robbie

Robbie just shook his head.

"How can we tell the girls their sister is not coming home?" I said. "What are we going to do?"

"I don't know," he said.

I felt so lost.

"We need to say a prayer," Robbie said.

I bowed my head, wondering how my life could go on.

Robbie's prayer was simple and to the point. We needed help. We needed God's compassion and guidance because we were lost and broken.

As he spoke, a familiar voice entered my mind. It was clearly my father's voice, speaking aloud the same words of comfort he had spoken so many years before: *Heavenly Father will never give you something you can't handle. He will never abandon you. There is always a way. Everything you need will be provided for you—everything.*

A powerful feeling of peace came rushing through my body, reassuring me that Emilie was all right. She wasn't afraid; she didn't feel any pain or confusion. God was promising me that He would provide a way for me to get through this, but in that moment, I couldn't see how. My life seemed impossible without my baby girl.

The drive home was quiet. I kept running scripts through my head, thinking what I could say to Emilie's sisters. Madeline was weeks away from turning five and Samantha was only three and a half. Emilie was their favorite person in the whole world, the leader of their little-girl pack, the one with all the fun ideas. What would it be like for them now?

Telling the girls was heartbreaking—first, because I could hardly believe the words myself, and second, because I could see immediately that the girls didn't fully understand what I was trying to tell them. It was hard enough to say it once— *Emilie has died and she won't be coming home again*—but to face having to explain it over and over again, to answer the many questions I knew they needed to ask, made me feel sick.

I had always believed in heaven. Because of my experiences over the years, I had studied and pondered, constructing and confirming my beliefs about death and dying. Especially after my father's death, I had built a sturdy boat of faith to sail above the sea of darkness and loss. But the reality of my daughter being cruelly stolen from me suddenly made me question everything I had ever believed. My ship of faith was rocking, and the dark seas of doubt began to rise. *What if I was wrong?* When the girls had left Robbie and me alone, I turned to him and cried, "It's all true, right? All the things we believe about death and God . . . it's all true?" I had to *know.* Faith just wasn't enough anymore. Robbie and I hugged, and I could feel him nodding his head yes. *Yes, it is all true.*

I needed a moment to myself. I walked into the bathroom and turned on the shower. In some way I hoped I could wash away the past ten hours. Emilie would still be alive, running around the house looking for her library books. The warm water splashed on my face. I imagined Emilie and what her final moments must have been, and, like a huge wave breaking, tears came pouring out uncontrollably. I couldn't stop crying. *Murdered! Murdered!* After a few minutes I heard the bathroom door open. It was Robbie checking in on me. He shut the door, and I heard him begin to sob.

That evening around 6:00 p.m. there was a knock on our door. Robbie opened it and found a tall man in a dark suit. He introduced himself as David Checketts, an area representative for the Mormon church. He had two other men with him, his assistants. They had come to offer their condolences and provide us with assistance for funeral arrangements.

Robbie invited them to have a seat at our kitchen table. All I could think about was that I had no intention of burying Emilie in Connecticut. We had no ties there. Besides, I wanted her buried next to my dad.

But I knew we didn't have money to fly Emilie back to Utah, never mind the rest of our family. We couldn't even afford the funeral. We had thrown every penny into our house, and our savings were gone.

"I don't know what to do," I cried. "I don't know how to pay for this."

Mr. Checketts stopped me. "I don't even want you to think about money," he said. "None of that matters. We will take care of everything."

Before he left, Mr. Checketts prayed with us. I can't remember a word he said. But when he left, I knew at least we had some financial help, and for that I was grateful. Still, I felt so much pain it was hard to think, hard to breathe, impossible to sleep. A few hours later, at 1:00 a.m., a state trooper knocked on our door. He confirmed that Emilie's body had been positively identified as one of the victims.

During the next few days, it felt as if a vicious hurricane was whirling around me and I was in the eye, lying immobile on the couch watching it go by, unable to do the slightest thing. Our parents, siblings, and cousins had arrived to help, and they all bustled around making phone calls, packing, answering the door, and, worst of all, . . . asking my opinion. It wasn't that I wanted to be surly or ungrateful, it was just that I didn't care. I didn't care about anything, other than the fact that Emilie was gone. So any questions or decisions I had to make irritated me.

There was a lot of discussion about how to handle the media. Reporters and photographers had been knocking on our door nonstop since the shooting. Our neighbors noticed, and they parked their cars at the end of our driveway and sent the reporters away. They also brought us lots and lots of food. I had barely eaten anything since Emilie died. I had no appetite, and I could tell it was worrying my mom. She kept encouraging me to eat something, but I would simply shake my head no. In some way I was glad I could feel hunger pangs. I wanted to feel pain. I wanted to feel horrible. To feel any other way seemed wrong.

I could smile only for my girls, even if I was merely pretending. They were busy playing around the house most of the time, but they would occasionally cuddle up next to me for a few minutes. They knew I was hurting, and I worried so much about how this was all going to affect them. They were my first priority.

During those first dark days, I kept myself isolated. Except for a small group of family members, I saw no one. Robbie and I could not bear to watch the news and subject ourselves to the constant barrage of coverage about Sandy Hook. So I was unaware of the outpouring of support and sympathy being made by thousands of strangers in my town, across the country, and even around the world. I vaguely understood that people wanted to help, but I was too numb to understand what was taking place around me.

One of the first gestures of kindness to penetrate the fog of my depression and shock happened while I was at home preparing for Emilie's funeral. I was tearfully looking through her artwork, trying to select a few drawings and paintings to display beside her casket. Even this small task seemed mountainous, overwhelming. Suddenly I heard the humming of an engine, followed by a splashing sound coming from the direction of the heating-oil tank beside our home. I went to the window and saw a hose stretched across our lawn leading to an orange truck with a big silver tank with the words "Hometown Fuel" on it. I was confused. Our tank was almost empty, but we hadn't ordered any oil.

Through the window blind I watched the oilman recoil his hose after topping off our tank. Still confused, I opened the front door and meekly waved. He approached and handed me a slip. The cost of a tank of oil was usually about $500.

"We're sorry for your loss," he said. "The oil is on us."

At that moment I was still in a state of shock. I was in a dark, dark place, and I could see myself sinking further down and down. But here was this oilman—a perfect stranger—showing me kindness. It touched me deeply to know that this man had felt moved to help me, anticipating my need and meeting it simply, with no thought of reward or payment.

I later found out that the oilman's name was Rich, and that he and his wife, Cindy, were the owners of Hometown Fuel, a small family business. I found this out when, a few days later, Cindy telephoned my home and offered to make dinner and deliver it to the house. I thought of the words I had heard in my mind on the day of the shooting, *"Everything will be provided for you—everything."* I began to see that God was actually there, sending small blessings all around me, helping to provide a way forward.

4

I HOPE YOU
BELIEVE IN HEAVEN

~~~~~~

I woke up Saturday morning remembering my real-life night-mare. I felt drained and I desperately needed someone to talk to, someone who knew what I was going through as a mother. I was surrounded by family who wanted only to help, but I knew they couldn't understand what I was feeling inside. I had an acute need to reach out to another mother who had lost a child at Sandy Hook, but I didn't really know any. We were so new to the community that I hadn't formed friend-ships with the mothers of Emilie's classmates. I didn't know the name of even one mother.

I went online and discovered that the names of all the vic-tims had been released. Scanning the list, I realized that all but one of Emilie's classmates were on it. My eyes stopped on one name in particular—Josephine Gay, one of Emilie's best

friends. I remembered Emilie telling me that her friend preferred to be called Joey. The moment I remembered her nick-
name, I was jolted by another thought. *Oh, no!* I turned and
looked at the birthday present wrapped in pink paper on the
kitchen table. It was a Barbie doll that Emilie had picked out
for Joey. Emilie had deliberated for forty minutes picking out
this present, and Joey's party would have been yesterday, the
day after the shooting. Emilie's invitation was still pinned to
the refrigerator by a magnet. It had an RSVP number on it,
along with the name of Joey's mother—Michele. Here was yet
another shock: Joey was gone too! I knew exactly how Michele
must be missing her! I immediately felt the need to call and say
how sorry I was.

I called, and as soon as Michele answered, I introduced
myself as Emilie Parker's mother. I hesitated, intending to say
how sorry I was that Joey was gone as well, but before I got
the words out, Michele said, "I hope you believe in heaven,
because they are up there together."

Her voice was so steady, so sure.

"They are okay," she continued. "And they get to celebrate
Joey's birthday party in heaven. That party is going to be better
than any party I could have planned."

We connected with each other immediately and ended up
spending the next two hours on the phone. Michele was a de-
vout Catholic and shared many of the same beliefs I had about
heaven and God. We talked about our shock and exchanged
what little information we both knew about the shooting.
Suddenly I didn't feel so alone anymore. I had found someone who instantly felt like a sister. Michele's family was in the

Emilie and Joey, drawn by Joey's sister

process of moving to Boston in only a few short weeks. She was planning on burying Joey out of state as well.

Michele and I talked a lot over the weekend. After one of our talks, I went to Emilie's closet and ran my fingers across the row of dresses hanging there. I couldn't fathom having to pick out what she would wear in her coffin. Finally, I settled on a long, white lace dress. It was a dress she had chosen to wear at a wedding we were planning to attend in the summer. Emilie was convinced she would be a bridesmaid and thought her white dress would fit the occasion perfectly. It took everything I had in me to remove it from the hanger for the last time. Then I neatly folded it, placed it in a duffel bag, and left for the funeral home.

Emilie's body had been delivered to a mortuary in nearby Ridgefield after her autopsy was completed. Before we arrived, the bishop of our congregation in Newtown had called to say that the church would take care of all the fees. "There will be no fee," the funeral director, Mr. Kane, had said.

He was emotional when he introduced himself. "I'm so sorry," he said, his voice trailing off. His eyes were red and he was fidgeting with his hands. He told us that in all his years as a funeral home director he had never felt so distraught.

We handed him Emilie's dress, and he invited us to take some time alone with her, but I had already decided that I didn't want to see my daughter in that state. My last memory of her was one of happiness and vitality; I refused to replace it with something else. While Robbie spent some time with Emilie, I remained in the hallway with Mr. Kane. He explained that he would dress Emilie and prepare her for transport to Utah. The arrangements had already been made with U.S. Airways. She would receive exceptional care, he assured me. As he spoke, all I could think about was her cold body lying in the cargo bay of a plane. I tried to stay present, to pay attention, but it was hard to focus.

When Robbie came out of the viewing room, Mr. Kane left us alone. Robbie broke down in my arms and cried on my shoulder. After a few minutes, I told Robbie that I had something I needed to say to Emilie. Still unable to enter the room, I pressed my forehead against the door and pictured my little Em lying on the other side. "I'm so sorry, Emilie. I'm so sorry I wasn't there for you. I'm sorry I couldn't protect you. I promised you I wouldn't let anything happen to you. I failed you. I'm so sorry I failed."

I couldn't get past the fact that I hadn't saved her. As a mother, I was supposed to protect her. That was my job! Instead, at the moment when my little girl faced a gun, I was obliviously buying her Legos. *Why didn't I feel something at that moment and rush to her aid? How could she have died and I didn't even know it, couldn't sense it?* I had promised my daughter that I would never let anything bad happen to her, and I felt I had broken my promise. I had let her down. I didn't know if I could ever forgive myself.

I got in the car and closed my eyes and asked Robbie to tell me about her injuries. I had to piece together all the information of her death, as hard as it was to hear. The sooner I accumulated the facts, I believed, the sooner I could find some understanding, some grasp of what had happened. But understanding still eluded me, and it would for quite some time.

5

PINK RIBBONS

~~~~~~

The night before Robbie and I flew to Utah for Emilie's funeral, I was in her room, punishing myself with guilty questions again. Alone, I looked at the flowers we had painted together on her walls. Then my mind drifted to my dad. When he had died, I had been so confused and angry. I had no doubt that my dad was in heaven, but, selfishly, I didn't want him there. I wanted him in Ogden, Utah, and in my life, where he belonged. I wanted him running marathons, playing with his grandchildren, and enjoying retirement with my mom. He had been taken before his time, and that angered me every time I thought about it.

Lying on Emilie's bed, however, I realized something for the first time: my dad was actually right where I wanted him to be. He was with Emilie. She had gone through something

Emilie walking with my dad

terrifying and horrific, but my dad was there to greet her when she passed through to the other side. In other words, he could do now what I could not do—he could take care of Emilie.

That was when it occurred to me that if my dad hadn't had his untimely accident, losing Emilie would probably have broken me beyond repair. As I looked around Emilie's room, I was overcome with gratitude that I didn't get what I wanted when I begged God to let my father live.

I looked again at the pink and black flowers above Emilie's bed and remembered what she said to me on the morning that she died: *Everything is connected. Can you see it? Can you see how everything is connected, Mom?*

The next day as we were getting ready to leave for the

airport, I was surprised to see a long line of police cars pull up in front of our home. Confused, I looked at Robbie, and he gave me a half smile. "I forgot to tell you, someone arranged to give us an escort to the airport. They will help keep the media away, too."

I frowned back at him and he laughed, knowing that would be my reaction. I hated to be the center of attention. I always have. Accepting help or drawing attention to myself when I am helpless has always made me feel uncomfortable, exposed, and vulnerable. But as I looked at all the police officers and their solemn expressions, my heart softened toward them because of their obvious kindness and concern.

When our plane arrived in Utah just before midnight, I was completely exhausted. A police car was waiting for us out on the tarmac; I was told they were trying to avoid any possible news crews waiting in front. We began the forty-five-minute drive from Salt Lake City to Ogden, Utah, on the freeway toward my old home—the home that would feel so different, so cold and strange, now that both my dad and Emilie were gone.

About ten minutes into our drive, Robbie nudged me to look out the window at an upcoming overpass. Someone had made a large sign that said, "We love you Parker Family." *Wow!* I was surprised that even in Utah, people were aware of what had happened at Sandy Hook. I still hadn't been watching the news; from my perspective, the shooting was not a national event but my private sorrow. As we continued down the road, we saw more and more and more signs. Then along with the signs we began to see little pink ribbons tied all along the sides of the road. At first there were just a few little clusters here and there, but gradually the coverage grew to a full blanket of pink

Ribbons for Emilie

on every fence, tree, house, and mailbox. Stunned, I watched in complete amazement as I realized how many hundreds and hundreds of hands had tied all those ribbons to comfort us and honor Emilie. Without realizing it, I was crying tears of gratitude. In that moment, home felt a little less cold to me.

Emilie's body had been transported by U.S. Airways from Hartford to Salt Lake City. The airline would not accept payment, but the real shock came when we arrived at the funeral home in Utah. The entrance was lined with flowers, stuffed animals, toys, and cards. It literally looked as if the contents of a toy store and a floral shop had been transported to the funeral home.

I looked at the funeral director and asked, "What is all this?"

"This is all the stuff that came with her," he said.

"This stuff came with Emilie's body?"

"Yes," he said. Then he handed me two cards. One said:

When life seems like a mountain that's too hard to climb . . .
May you find the strength to take just one more step.

It was signed: "Angels in heaven." There were more than a hundred signatures on the front and back from U.S. Airways crew members.

The second card said:

Hold On . . . Until You Find Your Smile Again.

It was signed: "US Airways Cargo, Phoenix, AZ." About one hundred airline employees had signed this one, too.

It turned out that Emilie's body had flown from Hartford to Charlotte to Phoenix to Salt Lake City. Along the way, all the crew members—on the ground and in the air—had added gifts and cards.

Then we got a call from one of our close friends. He happened to be on the flight from Phoenix to Salt Lake City. He told us that when they landed, the captain had informed the passengers that a victim from Sandy Hook was on board. Out of respect, the captain asked everyone to remain seated until her body was taken off the plane. Our friend said the cabin was silent other than sniffles. Then he looked out the window and saw the ground crew standing at attention in a single line as the casket was gently loaded into a hearse that was escorted off the tarmac by the Utah State Highway Patrol. Someone at the airport emailed us a screenshot from an airport security camera. I counted close to a hundred uniformed airline employees standing on the tarmac in the cold as Emilie came off the plane. The line of people standing in silence was longer than the length of the airplane.

A feeling of love filled my heart at that moment. I had been so anxious being separated from Emilie on our flights. I had imagined her being cold and lonely on the plane. Knowing that so many people had given her such love replaced that image in my mind. She had been cared for with great respect and tenderness. It was a precious gift of peace to my mind.

6

SAY GOOD-BYE, SAY NOTHING

~~~~~~~~~

The next few days were difficult and busy. People were in and out constantly, dealing with plans and arrangements. I didn't know how I was going to manage at Emilie's wake. I hadn't wanted to attend the public memorial that would be held the night before the funeral. Grieving in the public eye made me uncomfortable. When Robbie and I arrived at the funeral home that night, a line had already formed, wrapping around the building. People had come from all over Utah to pay their respects. The thought of greeting all of these people as I stood beside Emilie's little white casket made me nauseous. I couldn't bear to hear all the well-intentioned comments about Emilie. I dreaded even more the easily proffered "at least . . ." statements:

"At least it was fast."

"At least we know where she is."

"At least she is at peace."

I knew exactly what people were going to say because I had stood in a line just like this only a few months earlier and heard these comments regarding my father's death. This felt even worse, unbearable.

Overcome, I suddenly bolted from the chapel. In the rear of the building I ducked into a closet and closed the door. A few minutes later, Robbie found me in the fetal position on the floor, literally gasping for air. The moment he saw me, he knew I just wasn't ready to talk to people about Emilie's death. It was one of those moments when I needed my husband to be patient and empathetic. At the same time, he was hurting too. And he needed me by his side at the wake. We were both broken, but we had to stick together. Somehow, I had to get up and walk back in there with him.

He gave me time, and I reassured him that I would figure out a way to get through the wake. Sitting on the closet floor, I prayed: *Please. Please get me through this. I don't know what to say!*

One of the many lessons that I was learning in the depth of my need was how to listen for the answers that come from God through "the still, small voice." I learned to trust those feelings and impressions that came when I was pleading for help. In that moment in the closet, two words came to mind: *Say nothing.* I wasn't sure how to do that. How could I greet hundreds of people without saying a word?

I followed Robbie back to the viewing area and took my place beside him, next to Emilie's casket. A man at the head of the line approached, and Robbie greeted him. Then the man turned to me and said something. I nodded, but I didn't speak. He understood. From then on, it became easier. I ended up nodding my way through the entire wake. I barely uttered a word. Nobody pressured me to say anything, and I got through it.

People tell me that the funeral was a beautiful service, but honestly, I don't remember much of it. Robbie spoke, as did our friend Mr. Checketts and Emilie's cousin Caleb. A children's choir made up of Emilie's cousins and her younger sisters sang angelic music. Elder Quentin Cook, one of the leaders of our church, gave a sermon on the comforting precepts of the gospel—that Emilie lives and had been welcomed into the arms of her loving Father.

But his words hardly penetrated my mind until he paused and addressed them directly to me. He said, "I want to speak for a few moments to Emilie's mother. The unique challenge for those who have lost loved ones, as you have lost Emilie, is to avoid dwelling on the lost opportunities in this life. When we view through the wide and clear lens of our Father in Heaven's plan of happiness, instead of the limited lens of mere mortal existence, we know of the great, eternal reward promised by a loving Father and His plan."

That single phrase—"to avoid dwelling on the lost opportunities in this life"—jolted me to complete attention. Moments before, my mind drifting, I had been thinking over and over, *This is not what I expected. This is not what I expected for her.* I knew at that moment that Elder Cook was a messenger whom God had allowed to see into my heart and to understand my personal struggles.

He continued, "Please understand that no blessing of this

Samantha says a last good-bye to her sister

life, including those that would have been Emilie's in her maturity, will be withheld from this precious daughter. The Savior said, 'Let your hearts be comforted. Be still and know that I am God.'"

As we left the funeral and went to the cemetery, I continued pondering the words of Elder Cook. He had promised that no blessing of this life would be denied or withheld from Emilie. As I sat at the cemetery service, looking at Emilie's small white casket, I made a promise to God.

I vowed then that I would try to follow Elder Cook's advice. I would try to avoid dwelling on Emilie's lost opportunities in this life. I would grieve for Emilie and feel the sadness of her loss, but I would work toward letting go of my own expectations, my own plans for Emilie's future. I would try to trust that God had an even better path for her. But I would need God's help in understanding her new life, in knowing what God's path for Emilie looked like.

The funeral was hard, but I found many small, tender mercies surrounding the occasion. Losing my dad had been difficult; losing Emilie was crippling, and yet somehow I felt stronger for having gone through the loss of my dad. That loss had helped prepare me in some ways for the loss of Emilie. At the very least, I felt more prepared to make difficult decisions, and I knew how to go through the motions of public mourning. The news outlets covering the funeral were very respectful of our family's wishes. They stayed a deferential distance from the funeral services and gave us complete privacy at the burial site.

The streets were lined with people dressed in pink with homemade signs saying "RIP Emilie Parker." I recognized many faces from my past, but many were complete strangers, all there to honor Emilie.

Before we left Utah, there was an unexpected knock at the door. It was two of our dearest friends from high school, Alan Prothero and Brad Schultz. On the day Emilie died, they opened a Facebook page and began raising money to help our family. We sat down together, and they presented us with a large envelope containing hundreds of receipts of donations from all over the world. Shocked, Robbie and I flipped through the stacks of names and donation amounts. Brad lovingly said, "We want you to take this money and take care of your family. If you need time off work, if you need to go somewhere to get away, this money is here to help you." We were blessed to receive the outpouring of so much generosity from many wonderful people across the country. Feeling the special love of our friends—some old friends and some friends we had never even met—was the most precious gift, far greater than any monetary gift they could have given us. God had promised He would provide everything our family would need to get through this, and I could now see more of the ways He was fulfilling His promise.

Book II

AFTER

7

GOD'S HANDS

I knew that coming home to Newtown and trying to fit back into our ordinary life would be difficult, but I had no idea just how difficult. After a couple of weeks at home, Robbie resignedly went back to work at the hospital. His associates had generously donated their paid time off to him, giving him precious weeks at home with us. But finally it was time for him to return.

My continuing grief and shock made it almost impossible for me to function. I would walk into my kitchen to think about making dinner, but instead of cooking, I could only curl up into a ball on the couch and watch the girls play. I felt the need to protect myself by living in a self-imposed isolation. I rarely talked to anyone outside my inner circle. I stayed away from stores, people, and schools. I changed my driving routes to avoid certain roads that led to Emilie's school. I found it hard to connect with people and struggled to carry on normal conversations. I couldn't focus on anything for very long. I even had a hard time reading, as I had once loved to do. I knew these were all patterns of behavior I couldn't continue forever, but for now, this was the only way I could survive.

Everywhere I looked I saw reminders of the way my life used to be. Emilie's unfinished drawings were still on the table in our arts and crafts room. On her bed, still unmade from the last time she slept in it, was a box of toys she had been collecting for children who had no toys for Christmas. Even the little doors on the Advent calendar remained unopened after December 14. It was as if my life had stopped when hers did. I

One of Emilie's drawings

couldn't deal with the choices: *What do I put away? What do I leave in place?* Tasks as mundane as setting the table for dinner triggered tears when I would instinctively reach for five plates. Then I would lose my appetite when I saw her empty chair.

This was the first time in my life I felt incapable of taking care of my family. When Emilie was a newborn, the members of my church had brought homemade dinners for a week. Though I appreciated their service, I didn't feel comfortable accepting help. When my other daughters were born and the offers of dinners for our family were made, I declined. I enjoyed being the one serving others, but I had difficulty receiving help. But now, when the sweet people of my church congregation approached me and offered to provide meals for our family, I humbly accepted. I no longer had the luxury of maintaining my usual pride or independence. I knew I was broken and couldn't provide for my family. So, for over a month, meals were given to us almost every night. It wasn't just our church friends who brought food. Neighbors, Robbie's coworkers, families from Madeline's preschool, and many others kept us supplied.

The service we received was much more than just meals. A snow-removal service cleared the snow from our driveway all winter at no charge. A group of moms from Newtown came to deep clean my home. In the spring, a group of strangers came and built a new playground for the girls in the backyard. Hundreds of small acts of kindness were given to our family, which I will never be able to properly acknowledge.

Again and again I was humbled by how God's love reached out to me through the love of these kind friends, caring for me when I wasn't capable of helping myself. For so long I had prided myself on being strong and independent. I had focused on the importance of serving others, but I denied others the opportunity of receiving the blessings of helping my family. Only when I was completely broken could I finally humble myself enough to be cared for. When my heart was broken, it was also broken open to feel the love of all these helpers, which embodied God's love and made it manifest in my life. He continued to prove faithful to the promise He had made to provide for me.

8

A MOTHER'S PRAYER

In the meantime, I tried to direct what little energy I had toward my family. I could see a big change in both Madeline and Samantha. For Samantha, being away from all the crowds of people and back to what was familiar helped calm her moods. I began seeing the old Samantha again. It was a blessing that she was really too young to understand that Emilie would never be coming back.

Madeline, on the other hand, really struggled with coming home. Suddenly there were no distractions, no friends and cousins to constantly entertain her, only reminders of the sister who was gone. She became emotional and upset and anxious anytime she had to separate from me. She cried at lot at bedtime, missing her sister. She asked lots of questions about

Emilie and what had happened to her. I could tell it was now sinking in that her sister was really gone.

"Do you miss Emilie, Mom?" Madeline asked me one night while I was tucking her into bed.

"Every moment of every day. How about you?"

"Yeah, I miss her a lot. Mom, what do you miss most?"

I thought for a moment and said, "I miss holding her hand." The truth was, I missed everything, but her hands were something that had been on my mind a lot. As a mother, you are focused on keeping track of your children. You hold their hands as they cross the street. You protect them and watch out for them at all times. Now every time I held Madeline's or Samantha's hands, I couldn't help but feel that one of my charges was missing. I was learning how much the small things—like having Emilie's rough little hand to hold—were the ones that I missed the most.

Spiritually, I felt I was standing at the beginning of a very long road to understanding and peace, wondering if I had the strength and courage to walk that lonely path. I thought often of my father's favorite scripture: "There hath no temptation taken you but such as is common to man: but God is faithful, who will not suffer you to be tempted above that ye are able; but will with the temptation also make a way to escape, that ye may be able to bear it" (1 Corinthians 10:13).

It was hard to accept that my "temptation," my testing, was "such as is common to man." How many mothers, in fulfillment of their worst nightmare, have their child brutally murdered? And yet I knew that God was more powerful than any heinous crime, and that He could indeed "make a way" for me to overcome this. I truly wanted to overcome. I did not want evil to win out. So much had been taken from me by an evil act, and I was determined not to give that darkness any more power over me. I just had to exercise faith until God showed me that way, and then muster the courage to walk it.

Thankfully, it never occurred to me to blame God for what had happened. I never felt the need to ask Him, "Why?" "Why did you let this happen?" "Why to these innocent children?" "Why to my daughter?" I had already lived through many struggles and challenges in my life, and I never felt that God was to blame for any of them. I had learned this lesson from my father. Living in an imperfect world—a world full of flawed people—meant that bad things would happen, even to the innocent. My relationship with God and my understanding of my own purpose had been strengthened by past trials. I had a strong belief that good could come from hard times. I trusted God and knew in my heart He was not my opponent; rather, He could be my comforter.

And so I turned to Him for comfort in my darkest hour. As a child I had been taught—and my own experience had proven—that God had the answer to every question and the healing balm for every wound. All I needed to do was ask. I had a heart aching with the loss of my daughter, and I had many questions. I was at my lowest point, and I needed God's help. I closed my eyes and prayed:

> Please, please, help me, Heavenly Father. I feel so empty without her. Is this the life Emilie was supposed to have? Was this your plan for her life? It isn't the life I had envisioned. Everything I see reminds me of the life she will never have the chance to fully experience. I need help letting go of the life I dreamed for her and

Emilie at the beach

seeing what her new life is. I need to understand that she is okay and she is happy. Please, help me understand so I can let go of some of the pain.

I miss her so much every moment of every day, and I am desperate to be with her. I have never asked for anything like this, but please, God, can I see my baby? Can she come to me in a dream? I would be happy if I could just feel her. Anything! I am asking you sincerely to please help me know she is okay.

I finished my prayer and hoped with all my heart that God would answer. I knew I had to accept her death and trust in His plan for Emilie's life—not mine. Elder Cook's galvanizing phrase played through my mind, "Avoid dwelling on the lost opportunities in this life." I had faith that somehow I could do that, if only He could show me what her life had now become.

9

HE TOLD ME HIS NAME

At the same time Robbie and I were dealing with this leaden grief, feeling we barely had the strength to make it through each day, we were asked to attend dozens of meetings—meetings with the police, with school administrators, with Newtown officials. Along with the other bereaved families, we sat in crowded rooms, learning more and more appalling details of what had happened.

The picture painted by these grisly details gave me nightmares. Like an awful movie, I saw Emilie's death over and over again in my mind. Each time I learned something new, the movie would play again. I thought a lot about the fear and the pain Emilie must have felt. Many times I would insert myself into the story, imagining all the different ways I might have saved her. If only I could have saved her. I would have eagerly given up my life to spare hers. I wondered if there had been angels with all the children that day. I so hoped there had been. Was Jesus himself there with Emilie? Would seeing Him have comforted her?

A memory suddenly surfaced that I had forgotten long ago: Emilie was almost four, and for the first time she began complaining of nightmares. After bedtime stories, I would tuck her into bed and lean in to kiss her good night, and she would begin to cry and panic because she didn't want the bad dreams to come. I would hug her and comfort her, and we would talk about her dreams and how they made her feel. At the end I told her if she wanted extra help, she could say a prayer to help her feel better. A few weeks passed, and she complained less and less about her bad dreams. One day, while walking through Costco, Emilie excitedly remembered to tell me some news.

"Mom! Guess what! Last night I was having a bad dream.

Emilie's contagious smile

I said a prayer and Jesus came in my room! He made me feel all better!"

Shocked, I asked, "Jesus was in your room?"

"Yes!" she exclaimed.

"How did you know it was Jesus?" I asked.

"Because," she said with a smile, "He told me His name!"

As I recalled this long-forgotten story, the same feeling I had felt back then came rushing though my body. It was a fire burning inside my heart, confirming and consoling. I began crying as I realized that Jesus in fact *had* been with her the day she died, as He had been with her in one way or another her whole life. I knew that Jesus was with my Emilie.

10

LOOK TOWARD THE LIGHT

~~~~~~~~~

When we first moved to Newtown, we had been eager to attend church in our new congregation. I was pleased to see so many young families with children the same ages as ours. That first Sunday I sat next to another woman about my age, and she asked me the usual getting-to-know-you questions: *Where are you from? Are you renting or did you buy? How old are your kids?* When it was time to send my children to Sunday school, the woman beside me pointed out Madeline's teacher and told me her name was Terri Turley.

The minute I saw Terri, I was struck by her appearance. She was tall and slender, with long, brown hair and a gentle, serene countenance. She was one of the most beautiful women I had ever seen. Then the woman beside me informed me that Terri had lost her twenty-one-year-old son, Matthew, a few years earlier when he was serving a mission for our church in Argentina. He had been walking on a sidewalk when a drunk driver swerved and struck him. Matthew died instantly.

It was a terribly tragic story, and two things struck me about it. First, I thought that I couldn't imagine what I would do if I lost one of my girls. Second, I couldn't help thinking that hearing about the death of Terri's son was a sad way to be introduced to her. I soon learned that Terri and her husband, Scott, had one other son, Jeffrey, who still lived at home despite being in his early twenties due to his special needs. He sat next to his parents in church, smiling and saying hello to everyone he saw.

In those initial weeks in my new congregation, lots of women told me wonderful things about Terri. I couldn't help noticing, however, that the introductory conversations about her always ended with a reference to the tragic way her son had been killed. The drunk-driving fatality had become Terri's identity.

I didn't ask Terri about her son at that time. I was just grateful for the way she connected with my daughter Madeline. But the way I thought about Terri changed dramatically after Emilie died. Our first Sunday back in our congregation after the funeral was miserable. I felt like the eyes of the world were on me when I entered the chapel. I hated the attention. I didn't want people's pity, and I didn't want to see their sad faces. I just wanted to be left alone. I remember sitting down on our pew and immediately shuffling through my bag in search of things to occupy my daughters during the service. I told myself: *If I look busy, maybe people will leave me alone.*

When I looked around, I couldn't help feeling angry. The families surrounding me were whole. We used to be a *whole* family, but we weren't anymore. We were broken.

I felt a panic attack coming. Afraid I was going to lose it in front of the entire congregation, I stood to run out. Then I saw Terri Turley sitting next to her special-needs son. I sat back down, and the reality of my situation sank in. I had joined a club that Terri had belonged to for a number of years. We were both mothers who had lost children in unimaginable ways. She was probably the one person in my congregation who knew exactly how I felt at that moment. I didn't feel alone.

Thanks to Terri, I made it through the service. Later, when I went to pick up Madeline from Terri's Sunday school class, she pulled me aside and said, "If you and Robbie are open to talking, I have had some experiences that helped in my own healing process, and if you ever feel up to it, I would love to speak with you. There is no pressure. Please take your time."

It took me a while to get up the nerve to take Terri up on her offer. I was too consumed by sorrow.

One morning I couldn't get out of bed. That morning I called Terri. A few nights later she arrived at our home with her husband, Scott. Sitting on our living-room sofa, they told Robbie and me how they lost their son Matthew. He had nearly completed his two-year mission in Argentina. They had purchased airline tickets and were planning to travel there to pick him up. They even planned to tour Argentina with him so he could show them all the places he had served. Then they got word that a drunk driver had killed him.

"The pain that gripped our hearts," she said, "was beyond excruciating and seemed to suffocate any joy that we once knew."

I related to those emotions. I had been living them.

She continued:

> The night we received our devastating news, I immediately wanted to turn to the Lord. I wanted to cry to Him with all the anguish of a mother's broken heart. Then it occurred to me that He could have—and I thought should have—prevented it.
>
> Immediately I began to feel something—a darkness—welling up in me that scared me. I knew in that moment I had to make a decision: was I going to be bitter or keep a tender heart toward the Lord? I bowed my head and promised the Lord I would not become bitter. I knew that I couldn't turn away from my Savior.
>
> That night a dream came back to me that I'd had when Matthew was a preschooler. I dreamed I was in a room and all of a sudden darkness came over me. I remember feeling so frightened. I had never felt anything like it before. I didn't know what to do to escape. Then I heard a little voice. It was Matthew's. It was the first time I realized I wasn't alone. He said, "Mom, look toward the light and you'll be safe."
>
> It took all of my energy to lift my head toward the heavens, but when I did, the darkness left. When I awoke, I was so troubled. I wondered what could possibly separate me from my Savior.
>
> It was so startling being reminded of this dream all these years later, and it became clear to me that it was bitterness that would draw me away from the Lord. In that moment I felt safe, though profoundly sad, within the loving arms of my Savior.

Look toward the light

Then Terri told us that instead of canceling their airline tickets, they ended up going to Argentina, where they visited the places and met the people whom their son had loved and told them about in letters. They also went to the scene where Matthew had been killed. Finally, they tried to visit the man who was responsible for Matthew's death but were unable to do so. Instead, they met with a journalist who was amazed that they had not come to Argentina seeking justice. They told the journalist that they had forgiven the drunk driver and felt only compassion and concern for him.

That last statement pricked my heart. This was something I hadn't yet considered doing—feeling compassion and concern for the Sandy Hook shooter. In fact, I preferred not to think about him at all.

After her son died, Terri continued, she met with one of the leaders of our church, Elder Jeffrey R. Holland. In the meeting he asked if she had questions for him.

"Elder Holland spoke tenderly about our broken hearts. He said, 'It's okay to be sad. A piece of your heart is missing. It's missing because it belongs to your son, and he holds it until you are reunited with him.'"

She then looked at us and said with deep sincerity, "Keep your hearts tender toward the Lord, and He will visit you with comfort and a 'peace that passes all understanding.' If you choose to be obedient to the Lord's will rather than becoming hardened or bitter toward Him, He will be able to penetrate your heart in the same way that He blessed me with the answers to my questions. I have faith that angels will surround, comfort, and guide you.

"Before we go," she said, "I have one final thing I wanted to talk to you about. I want you to be able to have some personal time when you can do whatever you feel is helpful to your healing. My children are mostly grown, so my home is pretty quiet. You were forced into a very public life, which is incredibly tough. Being so public and trying to deal with the needs of your young children is such a challenge. I would love to have the little girls come to my home for a full day each week; this will give you quiet personal time."

Then she took my hands and said: "I am in a position to serve you, and that is why God puts us in each other's paths." It was such a selfless offer. My first instinct was to say no. But how could I not feel that Terri was an angel with a lamp sent

Samantha, Terri, and Madeline

to help me and light my path toward the peace she had already found? I nodded and gratefully accepted her offer.

Terri's words overwhelmed me. There was so much to take in and think about. Could I show compassion and forgiveness for Adam Lanza as Terri and her husband did for the man who had killed their son? If, like Terri, I focused on not being bitter and on allowing God to help heal my heart, would my faith help me find Emilie again?

A week later, Terri picked up my girls for the first time. She did this week after week, without questions. There were times when I did what she suggested—stayed in bed all day and cried. Terri helped convince me that this was perfectly fine. There was nothing wrong with me. I was grieving, and grieving takes time.

11

TO HELP YOU
THROUGH YOUR PAIN

〜〜〜〜〜

We had been told by a few Sandy Hook family members that the town had been collecting donations and letters sent to the victims' families and holding them at a warehouse in town. We understood that many people had been touched by the tragedy at Sandy Hook, but because we weren't following the news, it still amazed us to know how many people were moved to respond. It was hard to grasp that what for us was a private pain was shared by thousands of strangers.

Nearly a month passed before we made it to the donation center for the first time. I had heard that many things had been donated, but entering the warehouse and seeing it for myself literally took my breath away. The large building contained aisle after aisle of donations stacked floor to ceiling, with barely room to walk between the stacks. Toys, school supplies, letters, teddy bears, and paintings filled large bins around six feet square, each emblazoned with the name of one of the victims at Sandy Hook. The sheer number of those names still had the power to shock me.

We walked down the line reading each name, looking for Emilie's name. Not only was her box full, but the stack reached all the way up to the ceiling and had begun to spill over the side. I asked the volunteer who accompanied us why our pile was so high. She explained that the other boxes had been that full for all the families; we were just one of the last to come and collect. I couldn't believe what we were seeing! There were homemade blankets, drawings and paintings of Emilie, toys for Madeline and Samantha, books, crosses, letters, flags, jewelry, children's drawings, poems, music, Christmas ornaments, shawls, and many more things. We filled our van completely and had to make several trips back that day to finally empty our bin.

We carried all the boxes down to our basement family room, filling it. I wondered out loud to Robbie, "What are we going to do with all this?" That night, after the girls went to bed, we decided to start going through the boxes and sorting the contents. After hours of working, we had barely made a dent in the pile. My energy level was so low I knew we were going to have to pace ourselves. This was going to take a while. By the end of the week, our living room was looking close to the way it had before, but I was mentally exhausted.

I was touched by the effort of those who had sent us all these gifts, and I wanted to take time to read and acknowledge each message. I was especially stirred by the many offers of prayers for our family. I was filled with gratitude for the love expressed in the prayers of strangers. It was a completely new

The first load from the donation center

feeling for me, but somehow I could actually sense the power of so many prayers supporting and bearing us up, not abstractly, but in a real and tangible way. Blessings were all around me, and I was beginning to see where they were coming from.

After the shooting, I was shocked—the nation was shocked—to see the power and impact one man's evil act had on so many innocent people. It was hard not to feel that the power of evil was winning in the world. But at the same time, God's love had touched thousands and thousands of people's hearts and prompted them to take a stand against evil, to send some token of love and kindness. I was given the unique opportunity to be a witness to many of those defiantly kind acts. People from all different walks of life, all different faiths and backgrounds, wrote to us and to other suffering families with unified love and power. It was beautiful, and it helped me see the power of goodness again.

One of the letters that touched me most was from a seventeen-year-old artist. When I opened her package, I gasped at the beautiful charcoal sketch she had drawn of Emilie. The likeness was perfect and the drawing literally took my breath away. I pulled out the accompanying letter and read:

> My name is Lacey. First of all I am so sorry for your loss. At 17 I cannot begin to fathom the pain you feel and my prayers are with you. I am also an artist and enclosed is a drawing inspired by your daughter Emilie. On the day of the tragedy, I felt a strong feeling that I needed to use my God-given gift to help the ailing families in the only way I possibly could, which would be to draw the picture as a memorial to their loved ones.
>
> As I later flipped through photos of the victims of the tragedy, for some unknown reason, a young girl with piercing blue eyes really stood out to me. Her name was Emilie. Later, a link to a video of her dad caught my eye so I clicked on it. I saw an emotional father, describing his daughter as loving, and to my surprise, an artist who drew pictures and cards to cheer people up. This was simply too much for me to handle. I wept. It all made sense now. I saw a glimpse into God's plan.
>
> You see, I'd like to think this drawing is from Emilie and me. For I believe she was sitting in the lap of Jesus asking Him to do for you what she had done for so many others, to help you through your pain with pictures. He reached down to me and compelled me to do the work of Emilie. For that I am grateful.

Also your daughter touched one more life—my own. At the time all of this was occurring I was pleading with God to give me a sign on which path to take with my life: to be an artist, a path that was unsure and I feared, or to pursue a more generic career, that may not mean happiness. This is the sign I was asking for. I realized my passion is for art; it is what I was meant to do. Next year I'm attending Pittsburg State University and I'm going to major in art. I will always remember that little girl who inspired me to follow my dreams, that beautiful little girl named Emilie.

I read this letter over and over, wondering if Emilie would have turned out to be like Lacey—a talented young woman wondering which direction to take in life. Reading this letter, as well as thousands of others, I would see again and again how much Emilie's story had touched lives. It was so hard to

Emilie the artist

understand how this little daughter of mine, who never met any of these strangers, could affect their lives for good. But I realized that she and the other victims at Sandy Hook had become symbols to many. They symbolized childhood innocence and unconditional love—so much that thousands felt compelled to reach out to us and to others, validating and commemorating that innocence and love. Their deaths were also a poignant reminder that life can be short, so fragile that we must overcome the fear that prevents us from doing what makes us truly happy.

The next week, we stopped by the warehouse again, hoping to stay ahead of the pile. We were amazed to see that Emilie's bin was again completely filled. We filled up the van once again—and continued to fill it week after week for the next few months. Sometimes this avalanche of kindness became a bit overwhelming. I had to take breaks from the task just to refresh myself. I had friends come over to help me read notes and sort through the boxes. I wanted so badly to write a thank-you card to every person who reached out to us, but I could see how impossible that would be. It would take a lifetime to express the gratitude I felt for the upwelling of goodness and love that had buoyed up our family.

12

ALONE IN THE WORLD

One evening, I had finished tucking Samantha into bed and was curled up on the couch waiting for Robbie to finish saying good night to Madeline. A few minutes went by, and I wondered why Robbie was taking longer than usual. Robbie finally emerged from Madeline's room and looked at me with wide eyes. "What happened?" I asked.

"You will never guess the conversation I just had with Madeline." Their conversation had gone something like this:

Madeline: Daddy, how can we see Emilie again?

Robbie (pulling blankets over her): Where do you think Emilie is?

Madeline: She's in heaven with Heavenly Father and Jesus.

Robbie: You're right. So, Madeline, I think the best way to

see Emilie again is to love Heavenly Father and always make good choices. I want to be there too. Do you?

Madeline: Yeah, I want to go there too. But what about the boy who shot Emilie?

Robbie: How do you feel about that boy?

Madeline: I think he was probably a good boy, but he made some really bad choices.

Robbie: How do you think Heavenly Father feels about that boy?

Madeline (pause): I think that Heavenly Father loves him but is not happy with the choices he made.

Then Robbie began to cry as he told me, "Alissa, I could feel Emilie there. I could feel her there with Madeline. She was there."

I sat there shocked. When Robbie and I didn't know how to answer or help our girls, their big sister did. Emilie was there with Madeline, just as she always had been, helping and supporting her in a way I didn't know how to do.

Then I realized that Emilie was there not only for Madeline but for me as well. In my heart, I knew that Emilie was telling me to view the shooter in a different way, the way God would have seen him. I still looked at him as a monster. All the bitter questions that people often hurl at God after a tragedy, I aimed at Adam Lanza. *Why? Why did you do this to so many innocent people? Why to my daughter?* Madeline, with Emilie's help, wasn't angry or bitter. She managed to see that boy as someone God loved.

That night I prayed again for God to help me remove the bitterness from my heart and to help me feel closer to Emilie.

Emilie signing "I love you"

While I was on my knees, a thought came to me—go to the temple.

In the Mormon faith, temples serve a different purpose than churches. Churches are for Sunday worship services and weekday activities. Temples are for sacred events like weddings and baptisms, but we also go to the temple to pray and meditate, especially in times of trouble. It's a very sacred place. In the aftermath of the shooting, I had been too overwhelmed with grief to think to go. Suddenly, I felt compelled.

The nearest Mormon temple to Newtown was in Manhattan, across the street from the Lincoln Center. It took about ninety minutes to drive there from our home. I told Robbie I wanted to go right away. Maybe, I told myself, I would find some answers while praying in a sacred place.

We drove into the city a couple of mornings later. It was January 15, 2013—a month after the shooting. Inside the temple, we entered the room where people go to pray and meditate. I wanted so badly to connect with Emilie that morning. That was my goal—to feel something that reassured me she was okay. With Robbie beside me, I closed my eyes, bowed my head, and waited for that moment. As I waited in silence, this thought entered my mind: *You need to talk to the shooter's father.*

Confused, I tried to push that idea out of my mind. I wanted to focus on Emilie. The thought persisted, however: *Talk to the shooter's father.*

That answer wasn't at all what I had expected. I had been seeking to feel closer to Emilie. How would meeting with the shooter's father bring me closer to Emilie? What would I even say to him? But at the same time, it was bracing to have such a concrete, specific assignment. If that was what God wanted me to do, then I would do it, no questions asked.

I left the temple determined. As soon as we got in the car to go home, I shared my idea with Robbie. At first he looked at me with bewilderment.

I admitted that I didn't understand all the reasons why God would ask us to contact the shooter's father. But He *had* asked; that was clear to me. Besides, I reasoned that Peter Lanza was the one person with access to information that might explain why his son did what he did. Maybe he could tell us something from Adam's history or medical records that would provide answers. At the very least, this visit might give us—and all the other parents—some shred of understanding.

Robbie agreed and, through intermediaries, we reached out to Peter Lanza. A day or two later we were informed that he had agreed to meet. We were given his email address, and we sent him a simple message:

Peter,

Thank you for your willingness to meet with us. This event has touched so many people on so many different levels. Although Alissa and I have been grieving, we have also realized how difficult and different this experience must be for you. I am not sure what your schedule looks like, but we would like to meet with you and offer our sympathy and support.

You continue to be in our thoughts and prayers,

Robbie and Alissa Parker

He responded immediately. A meeting was set for January 24 in an office building in Wilton, Connecticut. It would just be the three of us: Peter Lanza, Robbie, and me.

That morning it was all I could do to keep myself together. The reality of what we were doing had set in. I was going to meet the man whose son had killed my daughter. The more I thought about it, the crazier it sounded. However, I was convinced that I needed to do this.

When we pulled into the office parking lot, I was filled with a mix of anxiety and anticipation. I followed Robbie into the building, where we entered an empty elevator. The doors were just starting to close when Robbie caught them and held them open for a man who was heading across the lobby.

Robbie's thoughtfulness made me mad. *Why does he have to be so polite all the time?* I thought. I wanted a few moments to compose myself, and here Robbie was holding the elevator for some stranger? *Ugh!*

As soon as we started going up, the stranger turned to Robbie and said, "I really want to thank you for being willing to speak with me."

My eyes widened. It was him! Robbie had held the elevator for Peter Lanza. I couldn't speak. I was practically paralyzed. Luckily Robbie said something to him. As soon as the elevator reached our floor, I rushed to the nearest restroom. Alone in a stall, I gave myself a pep talk: *Okay, you can do this. Just say what you rehearsed. C'mon. You can do this.*

We met with Peter in a small conference room. It was clear at the outset that he had never expected to hear from any of the parents, and he was genuinely grateful for the opportunity to meet with us. It was also apparent that he was full of anguish. His hands were shaking and his face was flushed. He was just as nervous as I was. Suddenly, what I wanted to say seemed so simple, almost stupid. Still, I started talking. I told him that we were religious people and, while saying a prayer, I had felt an impression to meet with him. Then I explained that throughout the grieving process there was one question that we ached to have answered: *Why did his son do what he did that day?* I let him know that we didn't necessarily expect him to give us the answer, but I felt he had the power to help us find the answers. He could, for example, release Adam's medical records.

Before I finished talking, I expressed my condolences for the loss of his son. Something I said opened the floodgates, and Mr. Lanza had so much he wanted to share. He began with some family history.

Peter and his first wife, Nancy, had two sons. Adam was the younger one, and he lived with his mother after Peter and Nancy divorced. Prior to the school shootings, Peter hadn't seen his son in two years. He had sent him emails and left voicemails, but Adam ignored both.

He had developed into a very different young man from the

little boy Peter had raised. They used to spend hours together playing with Legos and going on hikes. He said that at thirteen Adam was diagnosed with Asperger's, a syndrome that falls on the autism spectrum. He was put on psychotropic drugs. He went from specialist to specialist. Eventually he was removed from the public schools in Newtown and schooled at home. There he withdrew even more and was an unhappy, isolated human being. Peter knew something was wrong with his son. But he never saw the signs of what was to come. He left work early on December 14 after seeing news reports on television indicating that the shooter had attended Sandy Hook Elementary. When he got home, a reporter was waiting in his driveway. The reporter informed him that a member of his family was involved in the shooting.

At this point I realized that what was keeping me up at night was very different from what was keeping Mr. Lanza up at night. He wanted so badly to understand what had happened to his son. He wanted to know why. Like us, he was desperate for answers. All he could say was that his son's actions were "evil" and our statements were "a glimmer of light through the dark agony."

The meeting lasted two hours. When I first arrived, frankly, I didn't care what Peter Lanza felt. I was thinking only about what I felt. By the time we left, my perspective had changed. I was living with a horrible loss. He was living with something worse. I was surrounded by sympathy and compassion for what had happened to my daughter. He was blamed and despised for what his son had done. Peter Lanza was alone in the world.

13

FACE TO FACE

~~~~~~~~~

At night, lying alone together in bed was a sacred and precious time for Robbie and me. It was our time to talk, to vent our emotions, a chance for each of us to try to understand how the other was coping. A few days had passed since our meeting with Peter Lanza, and our hearts had changed a lot since then.

One night, Robbie asked me, "Do you think you could ever forgive Adam Lanza?"

I looked at him and answered honestly, "I hope to. What about you?"

He responded, "I am sure I will, at some point. Right now I don't know when or how to do that."

Meeting with Peter had helped us see Adam as more than just a murderer. There was a history behind his actions, a history I had never considered important before. I could see the many intractable problems that he'd had growing up and wondered how I would have responded as his parent.

I had received an email from a desperate mother who said that she had a child with problems similar to the shooter's. Her son often spoke about wanting to hurt others, saying he wondered what it would be like to kill someone. I could sense the anguish in her words. She wanted to help her son but didn't know how. Many of the resources that she had tried in the past had failed her.

I thought back to all the things Nancy Lanza had tried to do for her son and how many of the resources she sought out had failed her, too. It was clear in hindsight that she had made a lot of mistakes. But, I wondered, did she make them out of sheer exhaustion? Had it become so overwhelming to try to correct her son's behavior that she had enabled it instead? After a lifetime of fighting against the current of his illness, did she just decide to stop? These were all questions I would never have answers to, but at least I was starting to understand how difficult it must have been for her.

My dear friend Terri Turley had tried to meet face-to-face with her son's killer. I wondered, if given the chance, would I do the same? If I ever had the chance, what could I possibly say?

After Robbie turned out the lights to go to sleep, I lay in bed thinking about the shooter. I thought about an exercise we had been given in therapy to use when we most desperately missed our loved ones. We were to close our eyes, picture them in detail, and enter into a conversation with them. I had tried this a few times in my mind with Emilie.

I found it to be powerful and helpful but at the same time overwhelming. It unleashed emotions that were deep and raw. I realized that if I wanted to try to forgive Adam, I needed to make an effort. In that moment, I decided I would try to talk to him in the same way. I said a quiet prayer to give me the courage I needed, and then I closed my eyes and tried to clear my mind completely.

I imagined an empty room with dark, receding walls. I was sitting in a chair with my eyes fixed on the ground. Adam was sitting in a chair directly in front of me. I didn't lift my eyes from the floor because I didn't want to see his face. I knew my anger would overcome me if I saw his emaciated face and huge, haunted eyes. I didn't want to hear his voice, either. This was about me, telling him how I felt. My heart was beating fast and a tide of intense emotions started to flood my body, but I tried to push them back. I needed to be in control. In

Emilie's grave

my mind, I began to speak to him quietly in a flat, emotionless voice.

I just don't understand. I just don't understand how you could look all those innocent people in the eyes and shoot them. I think about each and every one of their faces and imagine myself seeing what you saw in their final moments. I just don't understand.

My daughter's name was Emilie. You murdered Emilie.

My body tensed, and tears began to run down my face.

She was my life. She was my light. Do you remember her? DO YOU?!! You didn't just take life from her; you took life out of me and my family. I HATE that you had the power to do that. I hate that you still have the power to affect me, and I want it back. I refuse to let your evil choices affect my happiness any longer.

My hands were trembling, and my voice was pitched higher, louder.

The problem is, I can't take back what you did. I can't bring my daughter back. I miss her so much. I pray, and I search for her and try to feel her, and I get nothing.

Anger toward Adam came spilling out. In that moment, I truly hated him. I shouted:

I am beyond irate! Why didn't you accept any help? I am furious that your mother enabled you. I am frustrated that your father wasn't involved. And most of all, I am angry that I couldn't stop you. Every day I drive on the road you took to the school that morning and every day I imagine what I could have done to stop you. I picture myself ramming my car into yours, knocking you off the road into a ditch. I picture standing in the classroom with a baseball bat, swinging it at your head and knocking you to the ground. I couldn't save Emilie!

My anger dissipated, and I was left feeling broken again, defeated. I spoke quietly now.

I have felt so angry and so confused for so long, and I don't know how to let it go. I don't know how to forgive you. Do you deserve it? I guess I still don't know. I don't know if I am capable of that kind of forgiveness.

I turned away from him, feeling conflicted and a little guilty. Was I not strong enough to forgive? Or was there something else I didn't understand?

I opened my eyes and wiped the tears away, drained and still confused. Forgiveness was going to take some time, but at least I knew that I wanted to let go of the weight I had been holding onto. I could see now that I had become comfortable in my anger and bitterness. Hating Adam Lanza felt good. But I could see now that hate and anger were limiting me from moving forward. Perhaps those emotions also limited my ability to feel Emilie, the one thing I wanted more than anything. Perhaps I was standing in my own way on the path to peace. I knew that I needed to somehow release myself from hate and anger in order to move forward.

14

HAIRY MONSTERS
AND TINY TEACUPS

~~~~~~~~

After Emilie's death, my relationship with Madeline and Samantha changed in many ways. There was so much I couldn't do for them that I used to do easily and naturally. I felt terrible about it, but I struggled to play with them. It reminded me too much of playing with Emilie, and I would become physically ill if I forced myself to try. I didn't sew anymore. I rarely went into my craft room at all. In fact, I completely avoided the basement, where the craft room and Emilie's bedroom were. So I watched as my girls played together, and I commented on what they were doing, but that was all I could give in the beginning. If I pushed myself too fast, I would pay for it for many days later with an emotional shutdown.

I began setting small goals for myself each day. It didn't matter how small the goal was—if I accomplished it, I allowed myself to feel proud. And if I didn't feel up to it, I would try again later. I was forced to have a lot of patience with myself. Nothing was quick; nothing was easy.

One day, feeling particularly frustrated with myself for not being able to do all the things I used to do, I started inwardly berating myself for being so weak. *Why can't you pull yourself together? What's wrong with you that it's taking so long to get up to speed again?*

Just then, my dad's voice came clearly into my mind: *Alissa, it all begins with how you talk to yourself and encourage yourself.* He had given me that advice when I was learning to run long distances. As a seasoned runner, he had taught me that success in running all starts with how you talk to yourself, how you use your words to motivate and push yourself farther. Hearing these words so clearly now, I understood that I had to apply the same strategy in learning to run a different race—the marathon of grief. I needed to have patience with myself, to be kind to myself in my struggles. This small epiphany helped me change my whole attitude about grieving. I had to take a longer view and to be kinder to myself in the meantime.

The girls were experiencing a lot of ups and downs, just as Robbie and I were. They tried group therapy for a while, but eventually we decided they needed more one-on-one time with a therapist. We found a highly recommended therapist who was known for using a lot of play therapy. To be honest, I didn't know much about play therapy. Madeline was to meet her first, and she and I went into the session together.

I assumed I would return to the waiting room while the girls had their session, but instead her therapist wanted me to participate. My stomach tightened and I could feel my anxiety building, but I looked at Madeline's excited face and knew I couldn't let her down. We began the first exercise, which involved Madeline telling us all about the bad guys in her dreams. We had to imagine all the different ways we could defeat the bad guy and win. Everything in me wanted to run, but I tried to stay focused on Madeline and what she needed. Madeline dressed up as the bad guy, a hairy monster who broke down the door to find me. I had to wait on the floor with balls ready to throw at the monster. *Stay present,* I kept reminding myself.

Madeline came busting into the room roaring and growling, and I quickly got the balls and began throwing them at her. She laughed and pretended to fall to the ground defeated. Then she ran over to me and jumped into my arms and informed me that I was now the bad guy. It was a long hour that really tested me, but I left so proud that I had finally played with Madeline again.

Samantha loved to make picnics. She had her own picnic blanket, food, and dishes galore. Every day I would find her in a different corner of the house having her own elaborate picnic with all her stuffed animals. One day I walked by Samantha on her picnic blanket looking really sad. I stopped and sat down next to her and asked her what was the matter. She looked up at me with tears in her eyes and said, "I don't remember what Emilie looks like." She covered her face and began to cry. I picked her up and hugged her tight and just let her cry.

Without thinking, I knew exactly what she needed, and before I knew it I was back in my craft room with my art and scrapbooking supplies. Flashbacks to the night before the shooting ran through my mind. Emilie and I had been working on a sewing project together while Robbie helped the other

Samantha's tea set

girls paint. We were all there together simply enjoying each other's company. I tried to suppress the anxiety and sickness I felt anytime I entered this room. I tried to focus only on Samantha. I opened up a storage box and pulled out two small, empty binders.

"Samantha, I have something for you and Madeline. It's called a memory book. We are going to fill it with pictures of you and Emilie. And then we will write in it all the stories you remember about Emilie, so you will never forget them. Do you think you would like that?"

"Yes, Mom! Yes!"

Together we picked out pictures and paper for her book and began to fill the pages. Samantha dictated and I wrote down her stories of Emilie word for word.

"Emilie and me were doing a tea party in the kitchen. Emilie chose it." The picture showed both girls sitting on chairs in the middle of the kitchen with Sam's little teacups in their hands.

As we flipped through the photos, my heart overflowed with appreciation for every moment we'd had with Emilie. Every picture captured a precious expression of Emilie's, images that seemed to be fading so fast from memory, even my own.

As we worked on our memory book, I was surprised at how much Samantha remembered. I thought back to the time when I found out I was pregnant with Samantha. I could see now the meaning of the impression Robbie had when I gave him that news. God had told him then, *It doesn't matter what you think. This is right. This is how it's supposed to happen.* If it had been up to us, we would have waited at least another year or two before

Sisters forever

getting pregnant again. If we'd had it our way, Samantha would have been just a baby when Emilie died. She would have no memories of her at all. There would be no words or stories of hers to write down.

I couldn't help but remember Emilie's voice in my head again, *Can you see how everything is connected, Mom?* I looked at Samantha and felt grateful for the gift she was to our family and for the time she had been blessed to have with her big sister.

15

A BIGGER GOD

~~~~~~~~

One morning about two months after the shooting, the girls and I were all getting on our shoes, heading out to school, when Madeline noticed the present Emilie had bought for Joey's birthday party. I had stashed it on a shelf in the laundry room and forgotten about it.

"Mom! Joey's present!" Madeline said. "We have to give Joey her birthday present! Emilie died and didn't give it to her and I have to help!"

My heart sank. We hadn't even told the girls that Joey had been killed as well. They had never asked if anyone else had died, and I had dreaded telling them. We had tried to follow their lead in doling out details about that day. We answered their questions honestly when they came up, in an age-appropriate way, but we tried not to elaborate beyond that.

"Madeline," I said, "Joey is in heaven with Emilie. They died together. I am sure Emilie was so happy to have a special friend with her in heaven."

I could see by the thoughtful expression on Madeline's face that my words were slowly sinking in. She looked again at the gift. Then, as if a lightbulb had gone on in her mind, she excitedly exclaimed that she had an idea. "Let's give it to her family!"

I hugged Madeline and told her what a good idea that was. Joey had two older sisters who would love to get the gift that was meant for their little sister. I spoke with Michele, Joey's mom, and she agreed that they would love it.

Michele and I spoke on the phone often. It was so nice to have someone I could confide in completely. We spoke to each other with complete openness about what we were feeling, knowing that whatever we shared would be met with equal understanding. There was no judgment between us. We felt safe together. Many of our conversations were about our daughters and their sweet friendship. Emilie loved Joey, and we often smiled thinking about how our little angels had brought us together.

Although Michele lived in Boston now, her connections to Sandy Hook still ran far deeper than mine. She had lived in Sandy Hook for many years and seemed to know everybody. Since Joey had autism and was apraxic, or nonverbal, Michele had taken a very active role in her schooling. She had been an elementary school teacher for years before having her three daughters. She knew Sandy Hook Elementary inside and out and was acquainted with all the staff, and even from Boston she remained well connected. She always seemed to have new information to share about the shooting.

Together we would talk endlessly about the questions we both had regarding what went wrong that day. We found it disturbing that the things that could have made the biggest difference to the children's safety seemed to be the most basic, simple things: windows that could be fully opened, PA systems that worked properly, and classroom doors that could be locked from inside the classroom. These small changes might have given our children a way to protect themselves or escape. They were issues we had both thought about vaguely before the shooting, never imagining they would become so crucial at our school—or any school.

It was a bit strange that, as intimate as we had become as friends, I had never met Michele in person. I had come to know her as a person with a beautiful soul, but I had never even seen her.

So I was just as excited as Madeline and Samantha when Michele's family came back to Newtown and met our family for the first time. Madeline excitedly handed them the Barbie doll that Emilie had chosen for Joey's birthday present. Michele's two daughters excitedly took the gift and talked about how perfect it was for Joey. Since they had lost their younger sister and my girls had lost their older sister, when they got together it seemed to fill a void they all felt. The girls paired off and played for hours together. It was magical to see the way they helped each other.

As for me, I discovered that Michele was just as beautiful on the outside as she was on the inside. She was short and petite, with beautiful long, blonde hair. She was vibrant, approachable, and easy to talk to. I could see why she knew

Meeting Michele

everyone. Though she was small, I could tell she was more than capable of holding her own in a crowd.

Michele sighed, "Meeting Madeline and Samantha is like a breath of fresh air. They are old enough to fully comprehend the death of their sister, yet young enough to trust God completely. They just warm my heart. Their energy and spunk is just like their sister's. It is strange how they talk as if they knew Joey personally."

I nodded, understanding exactly what she meant. Emilie had spoken so often about Joey that I felt I knew her as well.

That night Michele, Robbie, and I got into a long conversation about the things we wished we had known about school safety before Sandy Hook, and our desire to do something about helping others learn from our experience. That night, after Michele left, I couldn't stop thinking about how we could help others. How could we reach ordinary parents and ordinary schools with ordinary budgets, helping them to make simple changes to protect their kids? Then I started to wonder, what if we could really do something about it? My mind was racing with ideas about starting a website to help motivate and inform communities about school safety. I began taking notes, writing down all the ideas I was having. After a long night with no sleep, I called Michele first thing in the morning to tell her my idea. Michele was excited and felt just as passionate as I did about the project. We called a few other mothers whom we had heard speaking about school safety, and we created a nonprofit organization that we would call Safe and Sound Schools.

Michele and I worked vigorously. There were so many people willing to help. Most offered their services pro bono. For the first time in weeks, I was finally working my way out of the fog. I had an outlet to channel my emotions into, helping keep my frustration and anger at bay, and it felt amazing!

Getting involved with Michele on this project we were both passionate about was great, but I have to say that Michele had an even more profound effect on my faith. What impressed me the most about Michele was the way she carried her faith bravely, like a shield. She was not timid about her belief in God and her religious faith, and she referred to them often. My natural tendency was to shy away from conversations about religion with people outside my faith circle. I didn't know how my words would be accepted. I didn't know if I had the right vocabulary to speak of faith with others. Michele taught me to be more comfortable with being a person of faith, and to be unafraid to share my beliefs with others.

Following her lead, I spent a lot of time discussing spiritual things, not just with Michele but with many of the families who had lost loved ones at Sandy Hook. The unexpected benefit of attending endless meetings with the police, town officials, and school administrators was that I got to know the other bereaved families. Over time, we formed an unbreakable bond born of suffering and support.

Because Robbie and I did not live close to our extended families, some of these parents became like family. We got together as often as we could as a group, and it was only when I was with them that I could completely let my guard down. Our lives had become so surreal and crazy that it was hard for people outside of our circle to comprehend what we were facing. We trusted each other completely and even found a way to laugh again.

In this setting, it became natural to share our feelings about God, eternity, and our hopes for our lost children. Robbie and I listened intently as some of these parents spoke of answered prayers, of intimations that their children were near to them, of dreams that felt sacred and truer than truth. These stories expanded my mind, taking me outside my own religious experience to see that God answers the prayers of *all* the suffering who seek Him. He is a God who weeps for *all* who mourn, who speaks comfort in many languages, who is bigger than the biggest tragedy, larger than the largest need, capable of caring for any and all.

The testimonies and faith of all these friends expanded my faith. If God could help them find and feel their lost children, I knew He could help me find and feel Emilie. In His own time, in His own way, I knew He would answer my faithful waiting with the reward of reassurance.

16

BLESSINGS FROM A BLOG

~~~~~~~~

In the meantime, I knew I had to do all I could to get stronger and healthier. I had been actively going to therapy and trying every day to improve myself little by little. I was very serious about working through my anger and my grief in a healthy way. Only by doing so could I keep my promise to God that I would release my regrets for Emilie's lost opportunities in this life.

One thing I hadn't done yet was open myself up in writing. For a long while, the idea of writing sounded exhausting, too much like a chore or an assignment. But I knew that Robbie was finding solace by putting his thoughts and emotions down on paper, and something kept telling me I needed to write.

I also hated to think that my girls, so young when Emilie died, would grow up without memories of Emilie. I wanted them to know Emilie, and I had to reconcile myself with the fact that those memories would have to come to them indirectly from Robbie and me. It would be up to me to preserve our family's story for them. And in the back of my mind, I hoped that concentrating on this project for their future would help me soften my heart and learn to forgive.

I tried to brainstorm the best way to start writing. It had to be done in a format that I would actually stick with. For me, storytelling comes more naturally through photography. For years, I had loved taking pictures and chronicling our family's life through photos. I wondered how I could somehow merge both writing and photography into the same project. *A blog! I could write a blog!* Ideas began to flow as I thought about stories I would write and pictures I could take. *This could work,* I thought. Of course, I had some reservations. I still felt the need to protect my privacy, and I had mixed emotions about exposing myself to the world on the Internet. I decided to make the blog private for a while, till I knew how comfortable I felt about sharing my thoughts.

I spoke with a new friend of mine, Stephanie Nielson, who had the most amazing blog, *NieNie Dialogues.* She gave me great advice on how to stay authentic in my writing. For instance, she suggested I turn off the comment section of the blog so that I could stay focused on telling my own story and not be distracted by the reactions of readers. She also said she had a habit of praying before writing. I wanted to stay grounded, and her ideas were exactly what I needed to hear.

I called my blog *The Parker Five* to recognize that Emilie was still, and would always be, a part of our family. I decided to write on the nights Robbie was at work, which would give me something to do on quiet evenings when I normally would struggle to keep my thoughts from dark places.

My first post was titled "Our Family of Five." I wrote the story about our family preparing for our church's Christmas pageant. All three of my girls were going to be part of the Nativity scene. The children were allowed to choose what character they would most like to be. Not surprisingly, Emilie and Madeline wanted to be angels, while Samantha wanted to be a sheep. They rehearsed the song "Angels We Have Heard on High" over and over and over. When they rehearsed, I could hear Emilie scream over everyone else, "Gloooooooooooooooo-ria." She loved to sing, but I'm afraid she couldn't carry a tune.

During one of the final rehearsals, just a few days before Emilie's death, I stayed home to do chores while Robbie took the girls to the church. He sent me a picture of Emilie in her angel costume, looking very poised and sophisticated. At the time, it made me laugh because Emilie always protested that she was too old for dress-up, yet she still secretly loved it. I concluded my blog post by saying that Emilie was still and forever a part of our family, but now as our real-life angel.

I posted the picture that Robbie had sent me that night, which Madeline loved. When I finished typing the story, I felt lighter, happier, knowing I had accomplished this one good thing. Madeline now had more than just a picture—she had a written memory to go with it. I realized that this blog could be a powerful resource for my girls. It could serve as a place where Emilie's memory could live, and our family's journey through grief would be documented to help the girls—and me—in the future.

After writing on my blog for a few months, I began to see

Emilie in her angel costume

many unexpected blessings come from my efforts. Writing gave me the chance to contemplate many sweet and happy memories of Emilie. It gave me a place to work through difficult emotions in a constructive way. I also began to use the blog as a way to keep concerned family and friends updated on how we were doing, relieving me of the burden of either answering endless calls and texts or feeling anxious and guilty when I ignored them. Eventually, I took the privacy setting off my blog because it became overwhelming to individually invite each one who wanted to read my posts.

This was a terrifying step for me. I hoped that people would understand my reasons for writing and would be kind and considerate in their responses. I prayed that there wouldn't be any Internet trolls waiting to use the information in a hurtful way.

I was knocking a hole in the protective wall I had built between the world and myself, and I had no idea what response to expect. I should not have worried. What came back to me was an overwhelming tide of love and goodness.

Inside my wall of grief, I often felt isolated and alone in my suffering. How could anyone understand what it was like losing Emilie? But as I began getting emails in response to my blog posts, first from family and friends, and then from complete strangers, I began to see that I was far from alone. As I wrote about feelings of depression and sadness, family members wrote to me and shared their struggles with the same feelings. Cousins, aunts, and uncles opened up to me with very personal stories—stories I had never been aware of—about their own wrestle with depression. Even though my specific trial was different from the trials of others, I saw that others, with their own unique crosses to bear, often felt emotions, sorrows, and fears that were very much like my own.

Many strangers thanked me for sharing my stories. At first this was difficult for me to understand. I had been writing for myself. I had never expected or even desired that Emilie's life be remembered by anyone outside of my own family. But through comments on my blog, I began to see the impact that the tragedy at Sandy Hook had had on the rest of the world. The hearts of many were broken by the violent deaths at Sandy Hook, their sense of balance in the world shaken to the core. What I could now see was that God was using Emilie's story to share a message of love, hope, and healing far greater than I could have anticipated.

Here are just a few examples of messages I received that

demonstrate how God, through me as an unwitting tool, used Emilie's story to touch and inspire others:

Hello Alissa,

My name is Natalie. I have spent the better part of my day today reading your blog, in between breaks at work, during lunch. . . . Your words have touched me, and your strength inspires me. My heart and prayers go out to you. . . . I cried for weeks last December . . . for your little Emilie, and all the other precious angels that were lost that day. I have a little girl, her name is Alyssa. She just turned four years old and started pre-school, which was terrifying for me. She was beyond excited, but I drop her off with fear in my heart every single day. Your blog entry "running shoes" inspired me to write you. . . . I want to make a difference, make our schools safer . . . I don't know where to start or what to do. I just know that I want to be a part of something to make this world a safer place, a place where we aren't afraid to take our kids to school, or anywhere, for that matter.

I also want you to know that I pray for your family and all the other families often. Your precious Emilie will not be forgotten. . . . I am sure that she is looking down at you from Heaven, smiling, proud of what a courageous mother she has. She is Home. I pray that your burden will be made lighter, little by little, until that precious day when your family will be together again for eternity. How very blessed we are to know our Heavenly Father's plan for us.

Thank you for sharing your journey. . . . I am sure

mine isn't the only heart you have touched with your words.

Sincerely,
Natalie

✤

Alissa,

Ever since December 14th you and your little Emilie have been on my mind. I have watched your interviews, read your blog, followed your Facebook page and cried so many tears for you and what I can't even imagine you must be going through.

The fact is, Alissa . . . you have inspired me: to be a better mom, a more active parent and work to make a difference in my children's school.

You have been a vision of strength and yet still show the true emotion every mother feels for her child. Your little Emilie was the face that followed me from December 14th to the present. That little blonde-haired, blue-eyed girl shares a striking resemblance to my own little girl. So the day I saw Emilie's photos flash across my television my heart sank, I cried tears of heartache day after day. How could this little girl I didn't even know affect me in such a way. The fact is as a mother we suffer for each and every child that is lost. We see our own little one in the face of another, we cry tears that are not even present yet . . . but in the end the feeling is real.

✤

Alissa Parker: If there is one thing I want you to know it is that you and your beautiful daughter Emilie have changed so many lives, you have changed my life! You are my inspiration and my guidance. You are so completely amazing and give strength to all those who hear your story. My heart aches for your loss but I leap with joy in knowing there is such a woman in this world who provides the strength so many of us wish we could carry.

Thank you for sharing your amazingly raw and precious moments with us.

I wish you and your family nothing but the best!!

Your daughter has made a difference in this world . . . a wonderfully, amazing difference.

Yours Truly,

Penny

As I read these and many other messages, I felt loved, supported, and understood. And I felt awe at the work God can perform when we just listen to His promptings. I could see that Emilie's light was still shining brightly in a world that desperately needed light and hope. It was completely unexpected, but it was beautiful to see.

17

PURPLE BLOSSOMS

~~~~~~

I awoke one night to find Robbie sitting up in bed typing on his laptop. I asked what he was doing and he explained that he was writing down an experience he'd had before he forgot about it. Robbie was really good about recording his thoughts and experiences, and waking up to him typing was something I was getting used to. I went back to sleep. When I woke up the next morning, Robbie said he had had a dream about Emilie and wanted to share it with me. I opened up the laptop and began reading his experience.

I just had a dream. In the dream, Alissa, Madeline, Samantha, and I were all in a bed in the morning. Emilie was in our midst. I could feel her presence. Then she was there! I could feel her, see her, touch her, hold her. She was beautiful—older and taller. She was grown. She said nothing. Alissa saw her too! I just told her over and over, "You know how much I love you? You know how much I love you?" Alissa grabbed her and made her look at her and said, "Do you know how much I miss you?" I kissed her cheek and kept saying, "You know how much I love you." She then leaned back on the bed, and I kept my arms around her and put my head on her shoulder.

I thought to myself, *This is real, this is so real. I can feel her and I am not letting go.* My arms were wrapped around her tightly and I just kept telling her how much I loved her. Then she started to slip away. It was like my arms started to slowly feel less and less of her presence. I started crying and just said, *No, No, No, No, No, No, No.* I could feel myself slipping back into my reality. I knew I was, and I didn't want to leave that place. I don't know where I was, but I wanted to stay and hold her and love her. Then I realized I was back.

Alissa was lying in my one arm asleep. I did not have her embraced with both arms as I had with Emilie. My new reality came back—my world here without her. It was not a dream like I had previously experienced, but I don't know what else to call it. What I do know is that dream was real. I felt enveloped by the Spirit letting me know I had been given a special gift. I immediately thanked Heavenly Father for this experience. The Spirit touched me in a deeper way than it had previously. The feeling sat deep within my chest, in my soul, in a place that had never previously been touched in any way before this.

I looked at the clock through my wet eyes and saw that it was 4:13 a.m. I had been lying awake only thirty minutes before, not able to sleep. This was real. I know it was. I have never felt anything like it before. I am so thankful.

I finished reading and wiped the tears from my eyes. I was so happy that Robbie was given such an amazing gift. It seemed so hard to believe a story like that could be true, but I knew in my heart it was. Robbie's description of Emilie played through my mind, and I tried as hard as I could to see it for myself. Robbie's experience was very powerful and sacred, and I understood the sensitivity of the message.

As grateful as I was for Robbie to have an experience like this, I wanted one of my own. I wanted to feel Emilie near me and see her with my own eyes. For months now, that desire had consumed my mind. I was growing tired of waiting. At one point, in my desperation, I tried any little trick I could think of to bring on a dream of her. I would go to bed at night focusing as hard as I could on what Emilie looked like, hoping that if I fell asleep quickly enough I could dream of her. But I hadn't had even one dream of her since her death. I tried to remain optimistic that my time would come, but my hope was wavering. What if the answer to my prayer to see Emilie was "No"? Could I accept that? I didn't know for sure, but I wanted to do whatever it took to be worthy. I had to have faith.

A few nights later, I was on the phone with Michele. If anyone could understand my need, she could.

The gift of purple blossoms

"Michele, have you had an experience with Joey yet?" I asked.

"Well, I haven't seen any angels or messages in the sky, and I don't hear God talking to me, but I do have moments where I 'know' something—out of the blue—and at just the right time. When Joey's funeral mass ended and the sky filled with the most beautiful snowflakes, I knew she was grateful for the celebration we had given her and proud that we would carry on knowing exactly where she was. When the gardens of my new home began to blossom in purple, Joey's favorite color, the spring after we moved to Massachusetts, I knew that was for us. And when I wake in the morning feeling inexplicably close to Joey, I know that heaven is not so far away. My child is growing up in heaven. Suddenly it's not such an abstract concept. I can feel it close by. I am living my life here on earth with one foot in this world and one in the next, longing to be with her, yet rooted to my earthly life. It makes me so grateful for the gift of family, friends, and a little angel to walk alongside me on this journey."

I thought about the beautiful picture Michele's words had painted. I thought about Emilie growing up in heaven and wondered if she was walking alongside our family. Maybe she had been there all along, but I had been looking for her in the wrong place. I was waiting for God to send me some dramatic sign, something undeniable and unassailable. But perhaps He was simply whispering to me, and I couldn't yet hear it. Maybe I needed to look for her in the small miracles of everyday life. Could I learn to have eyes to see Emilie in the ordinary things, in the snowflakes and the purple blossoms in my own life?

18

STREAMS OF MERCY

Easter morning for our family had always been an exciting event: new dresses, Easter baskets filled with toys and candy, and a special church service. But I knew that celebrating Easter for the first time without Emilie would be especially painful. I steeled myself for the pain; I didn't want my sorrow to ruin the excitement of Easter for the girls. I had learned to get through these difficult times by stepping through them cautiously, focusing as hard as I could on nothing but the moment in front of me.

After finding and tearing into their Easter baskets, Madeline and Samantha got dressed for church in their new Easter dresses. We had church early in the morning, so we all quickly scrambled to get ready. I went into my room to dress—and to compose myself away from the girls. I sat on my bed

Madeline at Easter

looking out the window at the sun coming up through the bare trees. My heart was aching.

Soon I could hear Samantha, already dressed in her Easter dress, running through the house laughing and playing. I heard Robbie ask her if she wanted some music to dance to, and she squealed a loud "Yes!"

A few seconds later one of Robbie's favorite hymns, "Come, Thou Fount of Every Blessing," was playing on the stereo.

> *Come, thou fount of every blessing,*
> *Tune my heart to sing thy grace.*
> *Streams of mercy, never ceasing,*
> *Call for songs of loudest praise.*

As this sweet song filled the house, I was flooded with emotion. I couldn't help thinking of all the things Emilie was missing. She wouldn't be opening an Easter basket with her sisters. She wouldn't be trying on a "fancy" new Easter dress. She wouldn't be hunting for Easter eggs. Most of all, I was thinking of the things *I* would miss: Emilie's sweet smile, her hugs, the way her little body felt against mine.

Eventually, I found myself being drawn toward the music. I pulled myself together and walked out into the hallway. I saw my beautiful little Samantha, who was then joined by Madeline, swaying and twirling to the music. In that moment, something overtook me. An enveloping warmth of peace and comfort spread through my whole body. And then I felt her. I felt Emilie! Nothing could be clearer or stronger. I *knew* she was there. I breathed in the blessed sense of her. Grateful tears poured down my cheeks, and I felt such a release. All the pain and worry I had endured for months was gone for that moment.

I knew that Emilie was there dancing with her sisters as they had done so many times before. In that moment, I was blessed to finally feel all the happiness of those memories again, all the joy and the laughter without the pain of loss. Emilie was giving me the chance to see that our family would always be connected, through time and eternity.

> *Teach me some melodious sonnet*
> *Sung by flaming tongues above.*
> *Praise the mount, I'm fixed upon it,*
> *Mount of Thy redeeming love.*

Robbie walked up next to me and wrapped his arms around my waist, and we watched the girls dance together. For that moment, we were all there as a family, tied together eternally by the redeeming love of Jesus Christ.

The feeling faded quickly, but even after it left, I knew I had been changed forever, lit with a new light of hope. As we attended the church service that day, the Easter story had a new, more personal meaning for me. I found myself thinking not just about Jesus but also about Mary, His mother, and her relationship with her son. She too had lost her child, someone special and pure who had so much to give. She had also lived with the tremendous burden of knowing her son's fate from before His birth. She raised Him, loved Him, and taught Him—all the while knowing that He would be taken from her. I imagined what it was like for her to actually witness His death, which was carried out in the cruelest, most painful, most humiliating manner possible. She had borne far more than I.

I was filled with gratitude for Mary. I had come to feel deep in my soul just how great her sacrifice was. I knew that I could never do what she was called upon to do. And I knew that her sacrifice, along with the supreme sacrifice of Jesus Himself, was performed for one reason—to help me and *all* the suffering children of God.

I thought of a favorite scripture, John 8:12: "Then spake Jesus again unto them, saying, I am the light of the world: he that followeth me shall not walk in darkness, but shall have the light of life."

My moment of light on that Easter morning in my living room had been bought with an infinite price, and yet it was a simple gift. That Easter, God had helped me see that Emilie was still, and would always be, a part of our family. I also learned that these simple, beautiful moments—if we recognize them as a gift from God—can have the most profound and lasting influence on our hearts.

19

ANGELS ROUND ABOUT YOU

The blessings of Easter lingered, helping me to feel more and more like myself again. I was finally beginning to walk out of the haze that had enveloped me for months. I had more energy. I found I was able to play with the girls more. Robbie and I were making good progress in therapy, gaining understanding of our emotions and the importance of communication.

I also began to realize that, in my months of pain and preoccupation with seeing Emilie, God had truly carried me. In a favorite LDS scripture, God promises, "I will be on your right hand and on your left, and my Spirit shall be in your hearts, and mine angels round about you, to bear you up." I thought with gratitude of all the "angels" who had borne me up, carrying me compassionately to this point: church members and family, my Sandy Hook friends, neighbors, strangers, counselors, Michele, Terri Turley, even my deceased father. God had indeed provided all He had promised, and now I found I was able to walk a bit more steadily on my own down the path of faith that God was showing me. I knew that if I walked faithfully, He would show me even more about Emilie's new life.

Around this time, I received an unexpected letter from a friend in New Mexico. It was from Cici, the mother of Emilie's friend Arianna from her Albuquerque school. Emilie adored quiet, shy little Arianna with her beautiful dark hair and her love of kittens. After we left New Mexico, Emilie spoke of Arianna often. In fact, only a few days before her death she had been drawing a picture of the two of them holding hands. I remember being surprised that she remembered how to spell Arianna's name correctly.

With interest, I read Cici's letter, which explained that Arianna had had an experience after Emilie's passing that she wanted to share with me. I called her right away.

Cici began by telling me that Arianna had been devastated by the news of Emilie's death. She was upset for days, and her parents were very concerned for her. One afternoon, Arianna's father went to check on her as she was playing in the backyard. She was alone, but he heard her speaking. It didn't sound like the normal prattle of imaginative play. It sounded like she was in animated conversation with someone. When her dad asked Arianna who she was talking to, she looked up and excitedly said, "It's Emilie! She is here with me! She is okay!"

Cici and her husband were caught completely off guard, but Arianna spoke with such surety that their hearts were touched. In the following weeks, the same thing happened several more

Arianna and Emilie

times. Once Cici came into the room where Arianna was playing and asked who she was talking with.

Arianna said again, "It's Emilie, Mom. Can you feel her?
Sit here and be quiet. Can you feel her here with us?"

Amazed, Cici and her husband watched as Arianna's spir-
its changed and she became her old self again. Cici confessed
that she and her husband had been spiritually struggling in
the last year, slowly slipping away from church. But after this
astonishing experience with Emilie, their family had become
much closer, and they decided to return to church and work on
their faith again. She thanked me for having such a wonderful
daughter and said she thought of our family every day.

I sat there frozen, the phone in my hand. Arianna was
someone Emilie loved and cared for, someone Emilie would
likely be watching from heaven. It made sense that she would
be with her friend, comforting and helping her. Arianna was

such a sweet, innocent girl, I couldn't imagine anyone more prepared than she would have been to sense an angel's presence.

I knew that Emilie had always cared about those around her more than herself, and I wondered what all this could mean. Was she still comforting others? Was this her purpose now? A clear impression entered my mind: *This is her new life. I am answering your prayers.*

Filled with gratitude for this insight—that Emilie's mission was to act as an angel of comfort to others—I had an urgent need to understand more and more about Emilie's new life. I began talking to friends and family, asking whether their understanding of angels was similar to mine. I recalled a sacred experience my aunt had shared with me shortly after Emilie's death. At the time, my heart had been too battered to take in the story or understand its significance, but now it rang with truth and meaning for me.

My cousin Lora, a dear friend of mine from childhood, died from cancer at the age of twenty-seven after a two-year battle that included four surgeries, radiation therapy, and a great deal of pain. Several months after Lora's death, my aunt had a dream in which she heard voices outside her living-room window late one night. Peeking through the blinds, she saw a group of ten or twelve young women lighted by the streetlamp. She recognized Lora in the group, and also a longtime friend who had just passed away. The women would break into smaller groups, entering different homes on the street, and then reconvene together. My aunt could hear them discussing how they had arrived just in time to help those who lived in the houses, naming different people whom my aunt knew as her neighbors.

Joy and peace filled my aunt's heart as she realized that

Lora was not just "up there" in heaven having a wonderful life, healthy and active. She was also "here" among us, helping people with needs, taking care of the people she loved and cared about. My aunt told me that the experience enlarged her vision of how our loved ones will continue to live, love, and even serve us when they move into the next life.

I also began studying and reading anything I could get my hands on. I came across a sermon given by a church leader, Jeffrey Holland, entitled "The Ministry of Angels." It seemed to validate everything I was seeing on my own:

> From the beginning . . . God has used angels as His emissaries in conveying love and concern for His children. . . . Usually such beings are *not* seen. Sometimes they are. But seen or unseen they are *always* near. Sometimes their assignments are very grand and have significance for the whole world. Sometimes the messages are more private. Occasionally the angelic purpose is to warn. But most often it is to comfort, to provide some form of merciful attention, guidance in difficult times.

I had always believed that angels were among us, but to understand their role in such a profound way left me breathless. It was beautiful to know that this was Emilie's mission. She was always near. She was one of those unseen angels carrying private messages of God's love for us. She was a comforter, a guide, a minister of "merciful attention" watching over our family and others. I was so proud of Emilie and the important work she was doing. I felt honored to be a part of this miracle.

20

THE OTHER RIDER

~~~~~~

With a new peace in my heart, my thoughts kept return-ing to Adam Lanza. The last time I had allowed my-self to think about him, I was shouting and screaming at his imagined image. Opening myself to that explosion of negative emotions had not been easy. But I knew that, deep inside, I was still angry, and I wondered how I was ever going to be able to let that anger go.

I pulled out a card I had hidden in my nightstand months ago. I rarely looked at this card because I wasn't quite sure how I felt about it yet. It was from a relative of mine whom I loved and trusted. Months earlier, at Emilie's funeral, she had come up to me with this card. She informed me that she knew what she had written in the card might sound a little strange, but she felt strongly that I needed to know it. I took the card from her and walked into a quiet hallway and opened it.

She wrote that she was sorry for our loss and that her prayers were with our family. Then she wrote the words that challenged me the most: "There is no easy way to explain it, but I need to tell you that Emilie wants you to know that she was more worried about the shooter than she was about herself."

I reread the passage over and over, trying to see if I was reading her words right. Emilie cared more about *Adam* than herself?

For months I had held onto the letter, wondering if it could possibly be true. I knew that Emilie was by nature a compassionate person. She had always been tuned in somehow to those around her who were sad or in pain.

When Robbie would come home from work, she would always ask him to tell her about the babies he had helped in the NICU. Their discussions often led to him taking out old anatomy textbooks from college so that he could explain his story better. He always commented on how she would be an amazing doctor someday.

When we watched my dad run in the Boston Marathon, there was record-breaking heat. At the finish line, we saw many racers sick from heat exhaustion. While my dad sat on the sidewalk trying to recover enough to make it back to the car, a racer who was walking by suddenly collapsed headfirst onto the concrete in front of us. Robbie ran over to help as the rest of us went to find a medic. Robbie held the man's head still and kept asking him questions: "What is your name? Where are you from? What was your time in the race? Who is here with you?"

As Robbie attended to this man, Emilie went and knelt

"Doctor" Emilie

down next to him. She stared at him compassionately, then reached out and put her hand on his shoulder. She asked Robbie why he was holding his head. She noticed that he was bleeding and that Robbie had blood on his hands, and she offered to go find him a bandage. After a few minutes some medics arrived and examined the man. Emilie continued to sit there waiting while they got him loaded into an ambulance. After they drove off, Emilie walked over to me and took my hand. I squeezed her hand and asked if she was okay.

"Yeah," she answered. "I just hope that man is going to be okay. I kept saying a prayer so that Heavenly Father would help him."

Emilie was full of compassion and love. It seemed fitting that she would be more concerned about the shooter than about herself. Could I look at him with the same compassion as she had? I thought about all that I had learned about him. It was hard to look past the darkness in him; I could see him only as a monster. I didn't want to see him as a child of God, too. For months I had been resisting seeing him as anything besides evil. But the truth was, I could feel my heart softening. I couldn't help but wonder if this was what Emilie wanted for me.

I often thought back to the way I had found peace when my father died. At first, we really didn't know anything about the other rider who had clipped my dad's handlebars, causing his deadly accident. As far as we knew, he kept on riding down Strawberry Pass and finished the race. At first, I felt nothing but anger toward this other rider. Why didn't he stop? Why didn't he say anything to officials? Why didn't he come forward and take responsibility for what he had done?

Weeks after the accident, that rider contacted my cousin, who had been riding on a tandem bike near my dad. He explained that the collision was caused by a combination of factors. My dad had swung out to pass another rider just as a faster group came around a blind corner. The other rider thought he was clear of my dad, but their paths crossed, and my dad began to wobble and then crashed. His own bike nearly went out of control, and he didn't regain his balance until he had reached the bottom of the hill. He stopped and looked uphill to see what was happening, but he was told by his riding group to keep going. Finally, he flagged down a car and told the driver that there had been a crash and that someone needed help. Only later did he and his group learn how serious the crash had been, and he was devastated.

When I learned these things, finally seeing the accident

from the perspective of the other rider, my anger dissipated. Not everything was as it had seemed at first. I was angry with the other rider only because I didn't know his story.

This epiphany became significant in how I came to look at Adam Lanza. Nothing could undo all the harm and heartache he had deliberately caused. Nothing could bring back those innocents whom he had killed. These were cold, hard, inexorable facts. But at the same time, I came to understand that I would never know his whole story.

The more I read, researched, and learned everything I could about the shooter and his history, the more questions surfaced to which I would never find answers. No one could explain exactly what had caused him to go down his dark path—poor decisions, mental instability, his parents, his obsessions, or a toxic combination of all these factors.

I finally came to the conclusion that I would never know. I would never fathom what was in his heart. But God could. God knew how to hold him accountable. God knew how to judge him. That burden was not for me to carry; rather, it was for me to lay down at God's feet. It was not something I needed to grapple with for the rest of my life. I didn't have to judge. I didn't have to figure it out.

As I made this decision, a burden so deep and so heavy it had nearly crushed me was physically lifted from me. My heart burned with a joy so powerful it brought me to tears. I had learned it was possible to forgive Adam Lanza, and that the first step for me was to choose to simply let go.

21

EVERYTHING IS CONNECTED

~~~~~~~

Several months later, I sat quietly alone on Emilie's bed staring up at the flowers stenciled on her wall. Memories of Emilie filled me. This room, her room, had been custom designed by the two of us working together. We had picked the drapes, the bedding, and the furniture together. We had sewed the pillows side by side on her little sewing machine and hand painted the flowers on her wall. She had picked out the paint colors at the craft store, and we had stenciled them on her wall later that day. Torn inside, I took my camera out and slowly began taking pictures of every inch of her room. This was my final good-bye.

Robbie had recently accepted a job that required a big move for our family, back to the Pacific Northwest. We hadn't been looking for a new job, but this opportunity had unexpectedly arisen, and it was perfect for us in every way.

During the summer, we had taken a family trip back to Oregon to attend the wedding of Robbie's friend Jake from PA school. This was the wedding at which Emilie had assumed she would be a flower girl. To honor Emilie, Jake and his bride-to-be, Kristina, had asked if Madeline and Samantha would like to be their flower girls.

The wedding was just the break we had been hoping for, and I imagined Emilie holding the hands of her two little sisters as they skipped down the aisle with their flowers. Of course, she would be here for this special day.

During the party, I noticed Robbie was missing. I walked outside to find him leaning up against the building. He smiled when he saw me and wrapped me up in his arms. "You know what I was thinking about?" he said.

Flower girls Madeline and Samantha

"What?"

"I was thinking about how worried I was coming back to the Northwest. We have so many awesome memories from this area. Back when our family was whole and together, and we were absolutely happy. I was afraid that if we came back it wouldn't live up to the expectations I have in my head."

I knew how he felt. I remembered all the good times we had shared here and how much our family had grown in both size and strength. I too had wondered if it would still feel the same, if it could still feel like home, coming back without Emilie.

Then Robbie continued, "I noticed that for the first time in over six months, I was able to look people in the eye. I didn't walk around avoiding people and places. I felt like a normal person. Well, almost."

Newtown was still a town in mourning. Reminders of the tragedy were everywhere we looked. It was difficult seeing the date of Emilie's death posted everywhere: 12–14–12. It was on bumper stickers, on people's T-shirts at the gym, on buttons pinned to the checkout clerks' aprons at the store. You couldn't escape it. I trained myself to keep my eyes on the ground. People often recognized us and would stop to give us a kind hug. Everyone was well intentioned, and I knew none of the commemorative memorabilia was meant to hurt or offend me. All the same, it was hard to see the worst day of my life memorialized everywhere I looked.

"I feel like a weight is lifted off of me," I explained. "Like I can finally breathe easier here."

"Do you think we should consider moving from Connecticut?"

"I think about it every day. I want to leave, but I only want to if it's the right thing to do, not because we want to run away from our problems. I am sure they would follow us if we did."

We hugged again and went back into the party.

Visiting the Northwest again made us cherish it even more. It was the one place we had lived that truly felt like home to us. After the wedding, we spent a few days visiting our favorite places in Oregon and seeing some old friends. It was healing to see places that held so many happy memories for us. Remembering anything about Emilie was like Christmas morning. Memories were all we had of her, and we treasured those stories deeply.

One of the places Robbie wanted to visit was his old school. He wanted to thank the teaching staff for their support for our family after Emilie had died. Robbie's class had raised money to help us buy the burial plot for Emilie's casket, and many of his old classmates had flown out to the funeral.

The staff was excited to see us, and within minutes the program director had pulled Robbie aside in her office to talk. There was a job opening in the department, and she wanted to know if Robbie was interested. She also informed him that a NICU at a nearby hospital was also looking for a PA, and she would love to recommend Robbie for the position. We couldn't believe the timing. For years we had tried to find a job for Robbie in the area, without success.

By the end of the summer, Robbie had been officially offered the job in Washington, and we had accepted. I could feel our prayers for guidance and help being fulfilled yet again, and I was so thankful for all the blessings our family was receiving.

But as perfect as the job truly was, it came with a lot of tough decisions and steps that frankly scared me to death.

Were we ready to leave the other Sandy Hook families? Could we leave this home, these memories? Could we say good-bye to her room?

I could see that God was asking me to exercise faith in taking this new step. He was preparing a way for us to escape, and we had to have the courage to walk the path He prepared.

One of the most difficult steps for me to take was putting our house on the market. Both Robbie and I feared, given the very public nature of our loss, that gawkers and curiosity seekers would invade the house. We especially shuddered to think of strangers peering into Emilie's bedroom, which we considered a private, sacred space. So to create a greater sense of control and to preserve our privacy, we decided to pack up her

Preparing to leave

room and paint over Emilie's flowers. It would be a wrenching kind of good-bye, so I said a little prayer to help me through the next few hours.

After I had taken photos and videos of Emilie's room, Robbie and I carefully packed up all her belongings. We took down her pink bed and pink curtains, and the room began to feel different. It wasn't hers anymore. We laid the drop cloths down on the floor and painted her wall. I cried the entire time. It was awful and it was emotional, but we forever made the memory of Emilie's room ours and ours alone. Tough as that was to do, it was right, and it made us feel empowered. Besides, I knew that, even without the stenciled flowers, we would always be connected as a family. Our memories of Emilie would follow us no matter where we lived.

22

EMILIE'S SHADY SPOT

~~~~~~

Shortly after Emilie's death, we had been approached by a man named Bill Lavin, a New Jersey firefighter. In the wake of Hurricane Sandy, Bill and his team had decided to build playgrounds along the New York, New Jersey, and Connecticut coastline to give the children in the area who had lost so much something to enjoy again. After the shooting at Sandy Hook, Bill had an idea to build a playground in honor of each of the victims of Sandy Hook. We immediately loved the idea, knowing how much Emilie loved playgrounds—that would be a perfect gift to honor her memory. Bill asked if we had any preferences about the location of the playground. We told him we didn't care where it was built, but we did request that it have shade. Emilie loved playgrounds with shade and hated being in the sun. Bill loved that idea and said he would be honored to find her perfect shady spot.

Months later, we heard that Bill had found the ideal location. It was in New London, Connecticut, in a beautiful, scenic area with lots of trees. The construction was going to take place in November, one of the last builds before the winter months. The construction and opening were scheduled to take place just days before our departure to our new home in the Northwest.

Many family members and friends flew in for the event. All of my siblings and my mom were able to make it, and I was so thrilled to have them be a part of this project. Bill had been right about the location. It was beautiful! It was right along the water and had the most amazing view of the Long Island Sound.

We were told that this land had been a source of contention for many years in the town. The area had become a dilapidated park that was now used more for drug deals than for children's play. There were many conflicting ideas of what exactly to do with this land. Many wanted to sell it to the Coast Guard, which had a station adjacent to the park. Others wanted to sell it to a corporation or build on it. The people in the neighborhood fought hard to keep the park as an area for their kids; there was not another playground on that side of town. For years, there was contention in the town over what to do with this land, until it was decided to build Emilie's playground. We were told over and over again that Emilie's playground was finally bringing peace and closure for the town. They were so honored to have it there and thankful to use that land for the community.

I was so impressed by the volunteers who came to build the playground. Many students from the high school were there cleaning up the grounds. The children from the elementary school walked down during lunchtime to see the progress and bring us snacks and treats. Friends from our church, the community, and school were there helping in any way they could. Volunteers came from all over the country because they had followed my blog and knew about our story. It was all so tender and overwhelming.

The playground was designed around Emilie's favorite things. Her favorite colors—pink, blue, and black—were the colors of the playground equipment. Her drawings had been etched into the walls of the structure. Even the name fit perfectly: "Emilie's Shady Spot." It was such a wonderful two days. We had a ribbon-cutting ceremony, and all the children ran onto the playground, playing and ringing the newly hung bell.

Emilie's Shady Spot

After the day had come to an end, my mom and I sat down on a picnic bench watching the sunset.

"Do you remember that volunteer who lives across the water?" my mom asked. I remembered him. He had volunteered both days and was a kind, well-spoken man.

My mom continued, "Well, he shared something with me that he wanted me to pass along to you."

"Why didn't he tell me himself?" I asked.

"He said you had so many people waiting to talk to you, he didn't want to bother you."

"What did he say?" I asked.

"He explained he is a spiritual person and has a strong belief in God and heaven. Last night, he had a dream unlike any dream he had ever had before. He was walking up toward a large white building, and in the front of the building he saw a young woman. He explained that she looked a lot like you, but her hair was lighter. She was surrounded by young children, and she was teaching them. He could feel the love the children felt for her and she felt for them. They listened to her every word, reacting to the story she told them. After the story, the children stood up and walked back into the building, and he walked toward the woman. He asked who she was, and she gave a simple smile and said, 'I am a teacher,' and she turned and walked toward the building. He told me he had the strongest feeling that it was Emilie."

I wiped the tears from my eyes as I absorbed the beautiful image in my mind. My heart was filled with a burning fire, and I heard the words I had heard many times before, *I am answering your prayers.* All the stories I was hearing confirmed my understanding of Emilie's new life and purpose. She was still touching other people with her kindness and love. She was a teacher, a comforter, a friend. She was indeed a ministering angel.

23

BUTTERFLIES FROM EMILIE

~~~~~~~~~

With our moving plans set in motion, we faced the approach of December 14—the one-year anniversary of the shooting at Sandy Hook. We decided it would be best for our family to be away from Newtown, with all its poignant reminders, on that day. We booked a week's vacation on a sunny island, enjoying a release from the grip of another Connecticut winter.

We had a wonderful, relaxed schedule. We walked everywhere, going to the same activities every day, enjoying the same places to eat. Every day as we walked, I counted butterflies. In the middle of winter, it was a delight to see butterflies, but I never saw more than a few, maybe four to six each day.

I could never see a butterfly without thinking of Emilie. She loved butterflies. In the spring of her fifth year, I had taken

Emilie to a yard sale, where she picked out a butterfly garden kit. She was so excited about having a pet butterfly. I tried explaining that butterflies don't make great pets. Once the baby butterfly became an adult and emerged from its protective case, she would have to set it free. Emilie insisted her butterfly would be different. She was going to show it so much love that the butterfly would never leave her. All I could do was smile at her sweet confidence.

We set up the kit in her bedroom and spent weeks watching for movement in the chrysalises that hung inside. Finally one morning the first butterfly emerged. Within days Emilie had a bunch of them. The time had come to liberate them. Our whole family gathered in the front yard for the big moment.

Emilie pulled me aside and asked, "Do you think at least one butterfly will sit on my finger before it flies away?"

I knew that was unlikely, but I didn't want to dash her hopes. "You never know," I told her.

Emilie undid the lid, and one by one the butterflies flew out and fluttered above the yard. Madeline and Samantha were ecstatic, but Emilie had a flat, disappointed expression. Not one butterfly landed on her finger.

Fast-forward to the summer after Emilie's death. I was in the yard with Madeline and Samantha, and for some reason my mind drifted to the day Emilie set her butterflies free. While the girls played on the swings, I sat on the grass and thought about how badly Emilie wanted more time with butterflies that day. At that moment, I desperately longed for more time with Emilie. But that was as unlikely as a butterfly landing on Emilie's finger.

Suddenly I was jarred out of my melancholy thoughts

when Madeline leaped off the swing and ran toward me, pointing in the air. "Look up, Mom," she shouted. "Look up."

An unusually large butterfly fluttered above me. Then it landed a few feet from me. It was the most beautiful butterfly I had ever seen.

"Mom, I think I want to hold it," Madeline said.

"Madeline, butterflies don't really like . . ." I got that far when the unthinkable happened. The butterfly walked onto Madeline's open hand. I couldn't believe my eyes. In that moment I was overwhelmed with love and happiness. I felt Emilie again. She was here with her sisters and me, finding the sweetest, most tender way to make her presence known.

Madeline held the butterfly to her face and got an eye-to-eye

Madeline holds a butterfly

view of the insect. Then she turned to Samantha and asked if she wanted a turn. Speechless, I watched the butterfly pass from Madeline's hand to Samantha's. I couldn't believe what I was seeing, but my heart was full.

Then, on the morning of the one-year anniversary of Emilie's death, in a fragrant island far removed from cold Connecticut, the moment I stepped out of our room, a butterfly few right into my face. I smiled. *That's one,* I thought. After breakfast, my count had gone up to six. By noon it was eleven. By nightfall, my butterfly count had grown to nineteen!

As we walked to dinner, I told Robbie about the butterflies, and how I thought it was such a sweet way for Emilie to say "Hi" to us. Robbie just laughed at my excitement; I could tell he hadn't really bought into the idea that this was something significant. After all, I hadn't told him much about my odd habit of counting butterflies.

While we were waiting for our food at the restaurant, a loud, unmistakable song rang through the sound system, "WHO LET THE DOGS OUT!" Robbie's eyes went wide and I started to laugh. Robbie hated this song. He had always hated it. Emilie, on the other hand, loved it! She used to tease Robbie by singing it over and over again, knowing what his reaction would be.

"Now she is sending *you* a message," I said teasingly.

Robbie just smiled and we went back to our conversation until the song ended. There was a slight pause, and "WHO LET THE DOGS OUT!" rang out again. The song played through a second time! But it didn't stop there; it also played for a third time! "WHO LET THE DOGS OUT!"

Robbie, laughing, held his hands in the air in mock surrender and said, "Okay, okay! I get it!"

It was so like Emilie—on the one hand the sweetheart, on the other the tease—to find two perfect ways to connect with us on this difficult anniversary.

24

AN ANGEL TO OTHERS

~~~~~~~

We left Connecticut on New Year's Day, 2014, exactly two years from the day we moved in. Our house had sold quickly, within one week of our putting it on the market. We counted that a blessing, another way that God was providing for us. The approvals for Robbie's hospital privileges and the licensing requirements for his new job were yet to be completed, so we landed in Utah to live with my mom for two months while we waited. Madeline and Samantha were thrilled to be at Grandma's house once again.

It had been many years since we had first moved away from Utah, and there was something comforting about being back. On Sundays we would go to church at the same building I grew up attending. I had so many special memories in that building—happy memories of my dad and my family growing up. Other memories, like Emilie's funeral, were more difficult. But there were many familiar faces that I enjoyed seeing every Sunday.

One friend in particular I was happy to see was named Alyssa—like my name but spelled with a "y." Not only did Alyssa and I have the same name, but so did our daughters. Alyssa's oldest child was also an Emilee, but spelled with an "ee." Alyssa's older sister had been a good friend of mine growing up, and I enjoyed sitting next to her in classes and catching up.

One Sunday Alyssa, who was teaching a Sunday school lesson, shared some news. She was pregnant! Everything had been going fine, but that week she had learned there might be something wrong with the pregnancy. The doctor had noticed some fluid buildup on the back of the baby's neck. She fought back tears as she explained that it was too early to tell what was really happening, but that she was hoping for a miracle. My heart sank for my friend. I knew the pain of losing a child, and I didn't wish that pain for anyone.

I sat down next to Alyssa after her lesson and asked her a few more questions about the baby. As she spoke, I felt so much love and compassion for her and her baby. I had been in her place many times, wondering if the child I loved was going to live or die. There is no worse feeling.

As Alyssa continued explaining, I began to feel the intense and familiar feeling of Emilie's presence in my heart. She was there with us somehow. But I could tell she wasn't there for *me*. I knew she was there to be with Alyssa and her baby, to comfort both of them through this difficult time. Overwhelmed with emotions, I wept as Alyssa continued her story. The words came to my mind, *You wanted to know what Emilie's life looked like. This is an answer to your prayer.*

Again it was confirmed to me that Emilie was an angel, ministering to others. She was there to do the Lord's work by comforting those in need. Somehow I understood that this baby wouldn't make it, but that God still loved and cared enough to send comfort and love. I felt so proud to be Emilie's mother.

Later I would tell Alyssa about my experience in feeling Emilie comforting her baby, not sure if it would help. To my surprise, Alyssa told me how frustrated she was that everyone had been so focused on her and how she was doing, while all she could think about was her baby. She said how thankful she was to know that God was looking out for both of them during this difficult time, and that they were not alone.

A few months later, Alyssa delivered her beautiful baby

Our angel Emilie

girl, Ensley. She lived a few days and then quietly passed away. I wondered whether Emilie was there to welcome her back to heaven.

Emilie's life was not defined by tragedy, but by the goodness and light within her. She had been a light in our family for six years, and that light continued to grow and live on in a different way now. Again, God had answered my prayer to know what my daughter's new world looked like. I understood now what that future held for her. It was a blessing far more beautiful than I could have imagined.

25

A NEW LIFE

Our move to Washington gave us a fresh start, away from disturbing memories of Sandy Hook and close to the places where we had created beautiful memories with Emilie. We bought a beautiful little pocket farm with three tree-filled acres, a pond, a shed where we could create an art studio, and a chicken coop that we promptly filled with chickens. We named one of them Fancy, Emilie's favorite adjective. Here we hope to create many new and happy memories for our family.

Moving also gave me enough distance in time and space to look back at the year's maelstrom of events—some unimaginably horrible, some unexpectedly sublime. In all of it, I can see meaning, beauty, solace. I can see God's hand working through my life as He bore me up and brought me to this new place of peace.

Of course, some days are still difficult. I always feel the absence of Emilie in our family. I wear a bracelet inscribed with her name so I will never forget. One bereaved parent compared the loss of a child to the space that is created when you cup two hands together. No matter how tightly you hold on, the void is still there. But eventually, the events of a new life begin to swirl around that void, like a flowing stream surrounding a planted rock. There is happiness, interest, and beauty in your life again.

Getting to this place has not been easy or instant. It has required hard work and patience. Both Robbie and I spilled thousands of tears, spent hours and hours in therapy, explored our fears and feelings in endless midnight conversations. In our journey of healing we have prayed, and we have written, and we have become involved in projects of advocacy and activism. All of our efforts were necessary; all of them helped. But we could not have survived on our efforts alone.

We received kindness, help, and support from countless people. We were surrounded and borne up by angels from our own families, our Sandy Hook families, our neighbors, our church community, and the thousands of strangers who reached out to us in love. All these angels blesseded us and honored Emilie by their compassion and care. They were all messengers of God's love, a testimony to me that God was aware of our sorrows, and that He generously provided the care He had promised on that awful day at Sandy Hook, in ways that I never could have imagined.

My prayer to understand Emilie's new life was answered with an understanding so profound that it has truly changed my life and my perspective on the eternities. I was given a glimpse, through my own sacred experiences and the testimony of others, of her new life and mission as an angel to others. She serves now, as she always did, as a compassionate friend, a comforter, a helper, a teacher.

Looking back on her brief life, I can see how she was prepared for her ministering role by the amazing affect she had on so many people. I often think back to what her kindergarten teacher, Mrs. Brown, wrote to me when we moved out of New Fairfield: *Emilie is gifted. Emilie is going places.* She was right, of course. Emilie was gifted. She was going places—just not where I had planned. Yet during her short time on earth, Emilie had made lasting impressions on children and adults alike.

That same Mrs. Brown who had been Emilie's greatest cheerleader had been heartbroken by Emilie's death. Months later, she wrote to tell me of a conversation she had with "Parker-Parker," Emilie's kindergarten love, when she learned that Parker was about to move.

He had just put on his little red coat and was preparing to leave. His eyes lit up when he saw Mrs. Brown.

She hugged him.

"I needed to see you before I leave," he said.

She looked him in the eye.

"Emilie is gone," he said. "She's in heaven. Do you know she's gone?"

"I know, baby. I am so sorry."

"You know we were going to get married and be Parker-Parker and have lots of babies. We had a house and lots of rooms."

"I remember all the pictures."

"Do you think Emilie will know that I moved?"

Emilie and Parker

"Yes, of course she will. She will be watching you from heaven and the clouds."

"So she will be there when I move?"

"Yes, she will always be with you. She will be with all of us."

"I needed to see you because you are the only one who knows we were really going to get married. I needed to hear from you that she will be with me when I move."

"I promise you she will always be with you."

Parker smiled for the first time in a long time. Then he put his arms around Mrs. Brown, and they both cried.

Mrs. Brown recorded this experience and emailed it to me, along with this epilogue:

I will never forget that moment in my life. Seeing the power of love in a little boy was a true transformation. After that he said, "I am ready now; I can move."

Alissa, it was a moment that I will always be grateful for. I truly believe Emilie led me there. I will always remember it and your beautiful fancy daughter who knew the man she was going to marry at five.

The power of Emilie's love had a lasting effect on another stranger who came late as a follower of my blog. She reached out to me in an email more than a year after Emilie's death. She wrote:

Good morning,

My name is Natalie. I am a Connecticut resident who, like many, was devastated by the Sandy Hook tragedy. However, the wound has begun to open for me personally. On January 9, 2012, my fiancé and I were on our way back from our Las Vegas vacation. Our Southwest Airlines flight had a connector where we picked up passengers in Denver. Among those boarding was a woman with three of the most beautiful blonde little girls I'd ever seen. I volunteered to switch seats with an older gentleman after realizing that this mom had three children, one of which would not be able to sit with her. That was one of the best decisions I've ever made.

The child was a real "living doll" with the most gorgeous personality to match. My fiancé and I thoroughly enjoyed her. I have so many great memories of this lovely child. Although the flight was only four hours long, I felt like I had known her for years. I can't help smiling when I think of her "twinkling" nose whenever she smiled hard.

I always wondered how the family, which was moving from the West to Connecticut, made out. As I am now connecting the dots, I realize that you and the family I had been thinking of have so many things in common. I stare at the pictures (on your blog) with a flood of tears, telling myself: This isn't "my girl."

I would greatly appreciate it if you would email me with an answer. I haven't slept all night. I am a young black woman, who, at the time, had long hair and a black sweat suit. My fiancé and I sat on the left side of the plane. The child sat in the aisle seat so that her mom could still keep a good eye on her. The angel I was blessed to sit with graced me with an abundance of pictures and talk of "grandma's house." Once we landed, the mom was so appreciative of our assistance that she immediately introduced us to her husband and boasted of our good deed. The image of "my girl" waving good-bye as she walked in the distance keeps playing in my head.

Whether or not you are the family I was blessed to meet, my thoughts and prayers are with you and yours. If I can be of any support, it would be my honor.

Sincerely and respectfully,
Natalie

I read her email more than once. Could this really be the same woman who had sat beside Emilie on the flight when we had moved to Connecticut?

I wrote back, confirming that Emilie was in fact the girl that she had sat beside. Days later I got this response:

Good afternoon, Alissa—I must tell you that in the past few days I have gone through a sum of emotions. I've cried and screamed; become angry; prayed; felt confused; and wept some more. I began to question: What are the chances that I would come in contact with a child who would later fall victim to one of our nation's most heinous acts? Why me? How did this happen? There were over 200 passengers aboard that flight. Why did I go so far as to ask a few people to change seats to accommodate a mom in need? Why me?

As I watched you guys disappear into what would be your new lives, I remember feeling sad that I'd probably never see this beautiful butterfly again.

What I gained from all of my recollections was the answer my soul had been searching for. I now realize that I was "chosen" to be of assistance to one of God's most precious angels. I had been gifted the opportunity of a lifetime. I was blessed by God with the privilege to be able to say that I was in the presence of one of His angels, even if only for a short while. I thank God for what I first thought of as "strange irony."

Sincerely,
Natalie

My heart was overflowing. Natalie had recognized even then that she was in the presence of someone special, a "beautiful butterfly," one of God's "special angels." And just as Natalie was in a position to help Emilie that day, Emilie helped her, too, then and now, as her heart was touched with the tenderness of recollection. These special moments allow us to see that all of life is miraculous. With every person we meet, we may be "entertaining an angel unawares" (see Hebrews 13:2). God is speaking to all of us, every moment, of His all-encompassing love, but only sometimes are we privileged to feel it, to understand it. Emilie, with her sweetness and her innocent, open heart, often helped people to feel that love. She did then, and she does now as an unseen angel. I am sure of that.

For God has also answered my prayer to feel Emilie in my life, to know that she lives and is always and eternally connected to our family. Mostly, these have been quiet, private experiences, as gentle as an Easter hymn, as light as a butterfly's wing. Sometimes we felt Emilie in the most playful of things, like a silly pop song repeated over and over. But in time, when my heart had begun to heal and I was no longer preoccupied with mourning, I was granted a powerful, tangible manifestation of Emilie.

One night, I was lying in bed struggling to fall asleep. Looking over at the clock, I could see that it was 2:00 a.m. I had started thinking about writing this book, and I was worried that all the stories and memories I had of Emilie would be lost before I could write them down. I said a prayer that I would be able to remember these precious stories and record them for my family. As soon as I finished my prayer, memories flooded my mind: memories of my father and his wise words to me, memories of Emilie and all the happiness she brought to our lives.

Finally, the flood of memories left my mind. With my eyes closed, lying in my bed, I felt a strong burning sensation in my

Feeling the love of God

heart. My body felt heavy and I couldn't move. My left arm started to tingle, and I began to feel the now familiar sensation that Emilie was somehow with me.

In my mind, I could see that I was in heaven. It was the most beautiful place I had ever seen, with rolling hills of lush green grass, verdant trees, and patches of colorful flowers. I could see many people all around, dressed in white, but I could not distinguish anyone. It was as if I were looking through a scrim or some filtered sense, and I couldn't see anything clearly. But I knew that Emilie was standing next to me. I could feel her. Then, the tingling sensation reached my hand, and I could feel something squeeze it. It was Emilie, holding my hand once again. I was literally holding the precious, rough, artist's hand that I had thought about, had missed almost every day since her passing. I couldn't see Emilie because she was at my side guiding me. I knew I had been given this one moment to see what Emilie sees, to know what she knows: that heaven is beautiful and that it is her home.

Instantly, the vision was gone and I could move my body again. But my heart was filled with so much excitement and love that it felt like it would burst. I lay there in complete happiness and peace. Emilie was happy. I lay in my bed and began to cry with gratitude.

EPILOGUE

~~~~~~~~~

Recently, I went for a run on one of my favorite trails, a wooded pathway that circles a beautiful lake. I was struggling a bit, having taken a few weeks off from running. Determined not to quit, I kept pressing on, even when large drops of rain began falling through the trees and soaking my jacket.

For some reason, my mind turned to the shooter responsible for Emilie's death. Honestly, I don't think about him often anymore, although there was a time when I thought about him almost obsessively. The question came into my mind, *How do you feel about Adam Lanza now?* I thought about the hard work I had done to come to terms with my daughter's murderer. Luckily, God had laid out many small steps on the pathway for me to heal. I look back at my first milestone of forgiveness and realize just how far I have come, even since then. It used to be enough for me to know that God would judge him and justice would be served. But now I could feel that my heart had grown softer toward Adam. I cared less about the justice of God and more about His compassion, not only for Adam but for all of us.

In His own way, and in His own time, God answered all my prayers. I had prayed that I could learn to forgive Adam Lanza. This was one of the most difficult things I ever had to do, and I am touched that it was Emilie's own example that led me to want to forgive. I have also learned that forgiveness is not a simple process. It is a choice that needs to be made over and over again, with each fresh hurt and each missed milestone in Emilie's life. But I discovered that as I became willing to let go of my anger and judgment toward Adam Lanza, rich blessings of comfort and understanding flowed into my life. When I laid my anger at God's feet, I found Emilie again.

As I ran the trail that day, I considered how Jesus taught that all men must forgive. He pleaded with God to forgive those who were responsible for His own death. Those Roman soldiers pounded the nails in Jesus's hands and feet just as deliberately as Adam Lanza had fired into the classrooms at Sandy Hook. And yet, Jesus prayed for God's mercy toward those lost souls, *Father, forgive them, for they know not what they do.*

I rounded the last bend in the trail, heading for the final stretch. I thought about how grateful I was I could now tell my girls that, never forgetting Adam's horrific actions, I had not only forgiven him but had learned to feel love and compassion for him. I stopped running, shocked at the word that had just entered my mind. *Love?* Was that possible? It was. Overcome with this realization, I began sobbing out loud and praying to God in complete gratitude. With God, nothing is impossible. He never gave up on me, waiting and blessing me while I kept working my way to the point where I could feel completely released. I was amazed anew at how faithful and how powerful God truly was.

❦

One night not long ago, I was reading a fairy-tale story to Madeline and Samantha at bedtime. The story closed with the conventional ending for fairy tales: "And they lived happily ever after. The End."

As I closed the book, Madeline asked me, "Mom, are there any princess stories that don't have someone who died in them?"

I thought that was an interesting question. We began to go down the list of princess stories we knew, trying to see if there was one. Snow White? No, her mother and father died. Cinderella? Both her parents died as well. Sleeping Beauty? Maleficent? (Yes, we counted the evil princesses, too.) We listed all the stories we could remember and couldn't find a single one that didn't include a death.

Samantha then pointed out, "We are just like those stories too, Mom! We had someone die in our family, just like they did! It was so sad. But we are still living happily ever after! Just like they did!"

Her statement truly struck a chord in my heart. I looked at my sweet, thoughtful little girls and asked, "Why do you think we have a happy ending?" And Madeline looked at me like I was a little slow and patiently answered, "Because we *are* a happy family."

It's true. After all that we have been through, we are still a happy family. Madeline is happier than ever. She loves playing sports and making new friends. Samantha is happy and thriving at school. They are both healthy, growing daughters of God. They have an understanding of heaven and God beyond their years. They are a gift to Robbie and me. They inspire me every day to choose love and to have hope.

Emilie is and always will be part of our happy family. Her smiling face greets us in the family portraits on the wall. Some of her drawings are framed there too. But, more important, we have learned to talk about her with humor and with love, not forgetting the stories in which she is less than a perfect child. When we share stories of Emilie's kindness and love, we can also laugh about how she was perpetually messy, a picky eater, how she sometimes fought with her sisters. No matter the story, speaking Emilie's name brings light into our family.

Madeline and Samantha in our new backyard

Robbie and I have come to love our new life on our little farm in Washington. We have both been forever changed by Emilie's death, but we are happy because of the way God led us through our trial. Our present happiness has an underpinning of confidence that, by the grace of God and through the sacrifices of our Savior, we are all still connected to each other in an eternal family that will never end.

I used to worry that we would always be defined by the death of Emilie, that we would forever be known as "that family whose daughter was murdered." I struggled to find a way to *own* my own story, to honor my daughter and what had happened to her, without letting that loss—and particularly the actions of the shooter who precipitated it—define who I am. My kind friend Terri Turley, ever an "angel" to me, gave me a new set of lenses through which to look at this conundrum: whenever people mention her son's death, she considers it an expression of respect and reverence for her son. She doesn't hear gossip—only sweetness. I am trying to be as wise in my own situation.

Something I learned as a photographer supplies a useful analogy for how I have come to view the tragedy in my life. When we first moved to the Northwest, I learned to love overcast skies. I discovered that when clouds cover the sky, all the other colors of a landscape pop more vividly in my camera lens. The same principle is true in my own story: the clouds that have passed through my life have made the ordinary joys of existence more precious and more radiant. I take fewer things for granted. I am more grateful.

I find that I am more compassionate. I have learned through my own experience how to "mourn with those that mourn . . . and comfort those that stand in need of comfort." So many people did that for me, and I want to return the grace when the opportunity arises. Often that means simply sitting with the suffering person and listening. I sit with them, feel terrible with them, and resist the urge to offer platitudes or answers. Only time and God will provide answers, but I can offer a sip of cool water and a shoulder to cry on.

My marriage is stronger because of the things Robbie and I suffered together. We both had to find a way to speak our anger and frustration without hurting each other. We had to resist becoming bitter. We had to put each other's needs first, striving to understand before demanding to be understood. We still work at it constantly. The result has been a deeper and more intimate love between Robbie and me.

I have found more courage to become involved in a cause I care about. Safe and Sound Schools, the nonprofit organization I cofounded with Michele Gay, has grown exponentially. Our website materials have reached 20,000 school communities nationwide, and we have personally delivered our message to more than one hundred organizations.

Finally, my faith in God has been tested to its very limit and refined in the process. I had to learn to trust in His wisdom and in His timing. He promised that He would provide all I would need to make it through, but at times it was difficult to rely on that promise. I can see now that He fulfilled all of His promises, but not with easy answers. He answered in a way that challenged me to go to work, to get outside myself and my old, comfortable ways of thinking, to have faith, and to hold on. When I stopped needing and pleading, when I was ready to let go of my anger and my insistence on my idea of a "happy ending," God blessed me more than I ever could have foreseen. He reunited me with Emilie, confirming that the ties that bind her to me are eternal and tangible. And He gave me a picture of her new life that is awe-inspiring and glorious.

ACKNOWLEDGMENTS

~~~~~~

I remember the moment in January of 2015 when I told Robbie I felt I was supposed to write our family's story. The same notion kept coming to my mind and wouldn't leave. This story is very sacred to our family, and I wasn't sure I wanted to share it with anyone else.

Knowing that I am not a writer, I felt that writing an entire book, especially about such a tender part of my life, was an impossible task. If it were not for the encouragement of my husband, Robbie, and my counselor, Deb Checketts, this book would never have been started.

Deb introduced me to an amazing writer, Jeff Benedict. Jeff believed in our story and began collaborating with me to write the first chapters of the book. It was because of his faith and hard work that this book exists today. In finishing the rest of the story, I was lucky enough to work with another talented writer, Kristie Guynn. Kristie's quiet and always thoughtful perspective challenged me to get out of my comfort zone and to be bold. She became not only my writing partner but also a trusted friend.

Through all the drafts and rewrites and edits, Robbie and my mom, Betty Cottle, were by my side. They were always positive and encouraging. I also want to thank Jill Garrett, Brooke Prothero, "the Oregon Girls," Brady, Nancy, and the many others who reviewed the early drafts of the story for their attentive readings and their feedback.

This story shared not only my personal experiences but also the stories of many others. Thank you Nancy McPherson, Terri Turley, Michelle Brown, Cici and Arianna, and Parker's family for allowing me to share your stories. I also want to thank Tauna Idone, my Sandy Hook sisters (Trisha, JoAnn, Krista, Scarlett, Michele, Cindy, and Lynn), and my real sister, Jill, for sharing their perspectives on the journey we shared together. I want to thank Chris Schoebinger, Emily Watts, and the team at Ensign Peak for all their hard work in publishing this story.

A special thanks goes out to Michele Gay, my sister in grief, in nonprofit work, and in life. You will never know the strength and support you have given me in my darkest times.

There are innumerable people I wish I could thank for all the prayers, support, and love given to our family through these past few years. Your faith has lifted me up and helped bless my life. I want to thank the Newtown LDS Ward, the Sandy Hook School community, and our old neighbors in Newtown for supporting our family with meals, acts of service, and love. You are in our hearts forever. To Robbie's brother James and his wife, Natalie Parker, our support for each other during our bleakest times brought us together in a way that neither time nor distance will ever diminish. I want to express my gratitude to our dear friends Alan and Brooke Prothero and Brad and Camille Shultz. You carried so many of our burdens and showed us what the pure love of Christ looks like. Thanks to Marian Salzman and our friends at Havas World Wide PR for protecting our family from the craziness in the aftermath of the shooting. We also appreciate the countless pro bono hours your organization has donated to help our family create The Emilie Parker Art Connection and Safe and Sound Schools, so that we can share the love of Emilie's life with communities across the country.

Finally, I want to thank my family again for their unconditional love. Madeline and Samantha, you give me so much light. Robbie, thank you for being my steadfast, priceless partner through all of this. This is as much your book as it is mine. I love you so much.